P9-ANY-551

SAINT TERESA OF AVILA

A SPIRITUAL ADVENTURE

TEXT BY: PP. TOMAS ALVAREZ, CD. AND FERNANDO DOMINGO, CD.
TRANSLATOR: CRISTOPHER O'MAHONY

EDITORIAL MONTE CARMELO - BURGOS (SPAIN)
ICS PUBLICATIONS, WASHINGTON (USA)

CA-O
248.229
ALS

*Coat of Arms of the
city of Avila. Beautiful
bas-relief in stone.*

PROLOGUE TO AN ADVENTURE

The aim of this book is to describe the glorious adventure which St. Teresa of Jesus embarked on when she answered the call to found a reformation of the Carmelites. Through it the reader can join her on the roads of Castile, la Mancha, and Andalusia and share the pain and the glory of this new birth.

It was a noble venture, conducted in manner reminiscent of those saints whom Don Quijote met on his last expedition and who caused him to exclaim: "These saints professed what I professed — they do battle. But the difference between them and me was that they were saints and fought in Godly fashion, whereas I am a sinner and fight in human fashion."

In Godly fashion, but no less humanly for all that, Teresa travelled the roads, on mule-back or by wagon, building chapels and carmels. That was what she spent the last fifteen years of her life doing, and she had founded her first monastery in Avila five years earlier still. So her founding activity spans twenty years in all, travelling in sunshine and in snow, in rain and cold alike. She was forty-seven when she started and sixty-seven when death cut short her last journey at Alba de Tormes, just when her cherished dream of founding in Madrid seemed about to be fulfilled.

Before we embark on this journey, it is well that the reader should know something of the background: the grey years in which Teresa laboriously built her runway, the horizons and landscape in which her vision was formed.

Teresa was born in Avila on 28 March 1515 to D. Alonso de Cepeda and Doña Beatriz de Ahumada. When she embarked on her founding activity she dropped these two surnames and henceforth called herself Teresa de Jesús.

The family might be described as belonging to the gentry rather than the nobility, what the Spaniards called hidalgos. Don Alonso had twelve children, three girls and nine boys. In an era enthused with conquest, riches and adventure in the newly discovered Americas, not surprisingly all the sons sought fame and fortune beyond the seas. Their mother had died when Teresa was only thirteen and Juana a new-born babe, so eventually there came a time when Don Alonso, Teresa and little Juana were the only ones left at home.

From the balcony of the now nearly empty home Teresa's inner eyes travelled well beyond the skyline: to the Argentine where Rodrigo, once so eager to accompany her to death and glory at the hands of the Moors, died; to Quito and Peru where other brothers fought and died; to Mexico where friends of hers had been and returned. Her own physical horizons were so limited by comparison. There was her aborted effort to flee to martyrdom at the age of six or seven, they had estates in Gotarrendura, and a sister married some miles on the opposite side of Avila; these places were the farthest she ever travelled. Apart from where her flights of fancy took her, her world was a small one.

At twenty Teresa too left home. "I remember that when I left my father's house it was with such heartbreak that death itself would not be worse; I left absolutely torn asunder."

She was leaving home forever, going to the Carmelite monastery of the Incarnation just outside the walls of Avila. Another world, another home. Another family too, but a much larger one: some 150 in all, between nuns and boarders — young girls who hoped to become novices in maybe five or ten years time. The community was very poor, in spite of the fact that all the noblest names in Avila were to be found there.

Life at the Incarnation took its inspiration from Mount Carmel, with its stories and legends reaching back to the Old Testament. As a religious institution the Carmelites dated from the early 13th century. The monastery of the Incarnation, however, was no more than about fifty years old when it opened its doors to Teresa.

Two years of monastic apprenticeship followed. Then, at twenty-two, Teresa took her final vows. Shortly afterwards, she was struck down with a mysterious illness which slowly wasted her body and very nearly ended her life entirely. In the summer of 1539 she had a complete breakdown.

"I had a fit which left me unconscious for almost four days," she tells us, and, when she regained her senses, "I was in such a state that only the Lord knows what I went through: I had chewed my tongue to bits, my throat was choking me, I couldn't even swallow water, I seemed to be torn limb from limb, and was quite delirious. I was all curled up and unable to move... any more than if I was dead.... As far as I remember, I could move just one finger of my right hand'' (L, 6, 1).

This illness is the starting point of quite an important aspect of Teresa's life. You could call it her physical history, perhaps. She retained her natural beauty and charm, but from now on she would always be very delicate. One of her triumphs was to constantly rise above the state of her health and conduct her affairs from the command post of her indomitable spirit.

To regain her health, Teresa had to leave her monastery for a while. She also left it for the odd, short and exceptional visit. Mostly, she just lived at the Incarnation and her travelling was inwards.

The world Teresa set out to discover and conquer was the inner world of her own soul. She called her journey ''the way of prayer,'' or, as the title of one of her books has it, ''the way of perfection.'' The books of the Franciscan spirituals were her starting-point and she followed the road diligently right up to the heights of the ''experience of God.''

It was an uphill struggle, with periods of backsliding, of weariness, temptations to abandon the quest and return to the broad comfortable surroundings she had left. She even gave in to these and, ashamed of herself, quit the undertaking. She wasn't able for that unconditional fidelity to the inner call which beckoned her on to the fullness of life.

Teresa devoted a whole book — her *Life* — to the story of these ups and downs: twenty years trying to learn to walk!

Then her father died. This seems to have acted as a spur to face God again. Ten years of further uphill struggle followed. And then, at thirty-nine, she was suddenly there, so to speak.

Two events mark her arrival at the top: a very personal encounter between Teresa and Jesus, and the reading of St. Augustine's *Confessions.* Teresa regarded this date as that of her ''conversion,'' and associated it with those two events.

She had reached the wonderful promised land of ''experience of God''; it was 1554.

As if she had been born again, with wings and new life, Teresa felt inwardly driven by LOVE and the need to DO.

By the new light in her life she discovered the ''interior castle.'' She rediscovered the meaning of life, the beauty of things, the dignity of the individual, the sublimeness of friendship, the true scale of values in all God's creation, etc., etc.

The phrase, ''what I see is like a dream'' recurs several times in her writings. It was as if she had never seen or enjoyed things before.... Her hour had come.

The planning and execution of her first foundation, St. Joseph's in Avila, took from 1560 to 1562. That year saw her undertake her first long journey: she went to Toledo, and stayed in that Imperial City for six months. That brought her into contact with the high society of her time and marked the beginning of her world tour — a social world tour, that is, in which she gradually came to rub shoulders with people of all levels of society, all walks of life, and all kinds. Among them were bankers, muleteers, merchants, boatmen, beggars, bishops, sacristans, beatas, theologians, country curates, dukes and duchesses, princes and princesses, even a king and queen. To list names at this stage would be tedious; we will meet these people as their turn comes to share the stage with our heroine.

We are fortunate that at this distance in time we can look in on the world in which Teresa moved: in her letters no fewer than 1,000 people who crossed her path still parade before us.

Her social journey went hand in hand with her geographical travels, of course. When in 1567 she left St. Joseph's, Avila, for her seemingly endless journeys on mule-back or in her covered wagon, she had been enclosed for thirty-two years. Outside, the Castilian landscape was still the same: holm oaks, poplars, wheat-fields, fallow land and bleak moors. But the human landscape had changed radically. The sun had set on the empire and on the triumphal spirit of the generation of Charles V.

The new generation was nervous and tense; times were lean and problems many. The Court had moved to Madrid. The Council of Trent had come and gone. The wars of religion had broken out again in France, and in Spain the forces of the Inquisition were not a sign of well-being. The unity of Christendom and of Europe was broken and would stay broken. In Africa, the King of Portugal's odd attempt to revive the Crusades failed with his death. All of this pained Teresa in a very real way.

It was only now, in fact, that she really discovered Europe: France, the Netherlands, England, Germany, and the Lutherans became part of the ideal and perspective of her carmels. It was now that she became aware of the "great evils which beset the Church" and began to feel them as if they hurt her physically: "To worry about anything else seems ridiculous," she remarked.

She re-discovered America too at this time, as she listened to Maldonado's reports of the millions of "Indians" whose souls were being lost.

Her journeys were confined to her own country; the slow-moving wagons never covered more than 40 or 50 kilometres a day. They cannot be even remotely compared to those of St. Paul or St. Francis Zavier. She never even reached the shores of the Mediterranean or of the Atlantic. The nearest she got to the sea was the view of the imperial fleet hoisting sails in Seville.

But, as we've said, her spirit roamed freely in other landscapes and was open to the whole world. As she thought of America, she wrote: "Those Indians have cost me no little suffering." She felt keen pain over Spain's war with Portugal. She placed her hope in the universal mission of the Church on whose chessboard she was conscious that she was a minor, yet indispensable, piece.

Though Teresa was not destined to leave her native shores in person, or even reach distant parts of it, like the Basque country or Valencia, she would reach the lands of her dreams and of her prayers through her daughters, and her words would reach them too.

If this book had to trace the path of her writings throughout the world it would become a sizeable atlas, especially if account were taken of all the languages into which they have been translated. In a way, I suppose Teresa is still travelling the world, dispensing her spirit in the bread of her WORD.

Autograph of St. Teresa. She begins the account of the foundation of St. Joseph's (Life 32): "Chapter XXXII: tells how the Lord was pleased to carry her in spirit to a place in hell which she had merited for her sins. Describes a part of what was shown to her there. Begins to tell of the way and means whereby the convent of St. Joseph, where she is now, was founded."

Avila, in the heart of the Iberian Peninsula. 111 km from Madrid.

AVILA

Dates and events
Site of the first foundation: Avila

1560 Two mystical graces: the vision of Christ and another, of Hell, recounted by Teresa in Life 27 and Life 32.

1560 Spring-summer: gathering of friends in Mother Teresa's cell in the Incarnation: origin of the idea of founding a poor convent.

1560 August 4th: Don Alvaro de Mendoza was appointed Bishop of Avila.

1561 August 15th: the Virgin Mary made promises to Teresa.

1561 December: Teresa's brother Lorenzo sent her money from Quito (Ecuador). A letter from the Saint to him (23/12/1561). The provincial ordered her to travel to Toledo (24/12/1561).

1562 Six months in Toledo, in the mansion of Doña Luisa de la Cerda.

1562 Teresa obtained a brief to found from the Holy Penitentiary in Rome.

1562 June: The Saint concluded the first version of her Life, in Toledo.

1562 August 24th: inauguration of St. Joseph's carmel. Summoned by the prioress of the Incarnation, Teresa left the new convent.

1562 August 25th: Avila Council began its suit against the foundation. Aug. 29th: "all the estates of the city" were required to oppose Mother Teresa and her convent.

1562 October 19th: death of St. Peter of Alcántara.

1562 December 5th: the Saint was conceded the Brief of Poverty in Rome.

1562 December 6th: death of the Order's General, Nicolás Audet. Juan Bautista Rubeo succeeded him as Vicar (29/12); he was elected General on May 21st 1564.

1563 July 23rd: Teresa's friend María de Jesús founded La Imagen carmel in Alcalá.

1563 August 22nd: the provincial granted the Saint permission to reside at St. Joseph's.

1565 July 17th: Pius IV's bull in favour of St. Joseph's.

1565 Last months: the final version of her Life was concluded.

… Important contemporary events

1558 Death of the Emperor Charles V, at Yuste.

1559 The Inquisition published the Index of Forbidden Books (by Valdés), including many of those used by Mother Teresa.

1562 Vassy massacre. Religious wars broke out again in France.

1562-1563 Last phase of the Council of Trent.

1563 Start of building work on El Escorial.

External view of St. Joseph's Monastery; drawing by Hye Hoys (1866-1867).

AVILA
ST. JOSEPH'S MONASTERY
24.8.1562·

Here is the first monastery founded by St. Teresa. It looks like a scale model of its more grandiose contem-poraries. One might say it was planned according to the scale of the Gospel; and, indeed, the Master's various comparisons of the Kingdom fit it admirably: the mustard seed, the leaven, the light on the lamp-stand, the salt of the earth, etc.

The river of history has many sources, all of them well-known, but they are all fed from ch. 32 of St. Teresa's own autobiography — the *Life.* It begins: "After the Lord had been granting me the favours I have been speaking of, and many others, for quite some time, I was praying one day when suddenly, I know not how, I seemed to be plunged into Hell" (L.32,1).

Convent of Our Lady of Grace (Augustines), which received young Teresa at the age of 15 or 16.

Façade of the convent of Carmelite friars in Avila (known as "La Santa").

Just as we appreciate the beauty of light only by contrast with darkness, or the gift of health only when faced with tragic illness, so Teresa, faced with this terrifying vision, decided to leave behind all deviation from the straight path, to flee the compromises of life, and devote herself wholeheartedly to being grateful for her own salvation and to bringing others to it.

Hardships were hardly noticed any more. "I find everything easy," she said, "compared to one moment of what I suffered there... I would gladly give a thousand lives to spare even one person such terrible torments" (Ibid).

Some means had to be found, and quickly, to avoid such evil and procure so great a good. She found it. Teresa would begin by reforming herself, by being fully consistent with her Carmelite vocation, by observing the Rule with all the perfection of which she was capable.

Let us be more specific. Teresa realised that living in the monastery of the Incarnation with some 180 nuns was like belonging to a respectable club. They were good women, of course, even servants of God; but nothing more. Good intentions are not enough for self reform. Social pressures make themselves felt in the monastery and come from the city outside. The nuns find a thousand and one perfectly lawful reasons for going and coming with the same frequency as the multitude of visitors who are always about the place. They have permission, too, to observe a mitigated version of the Rule. The monastery, to quote Teresa herself, "is a pretty comfortable place, being large and spacious" (Ibid).

Besides, Teresa was not the only one to feel the way she did about things. She had often discussed the state of the monastery with her close friends. And, finally, one September evening in 1560, those friends and relations — some of them nuns and some lay people — were together again in Teresa's cell. No doubt they talked of many things, but inevitably their

Overall view of the monastery of the Incarnation, where Teresa became a Carmelite.

favourite topic came up again: the need for more solitude, their desire for a new style of monastic life. A community of well over a hundred nuns, they felt, was not conducive to the intimate fraternity of all, free from cliques and the impersonal environment created by a structure of government designed for large numbers. They were also convinced that so much contact with outsiders was not exactly a help. A young nun called María de Ocampo, a niece of St. Teresa's, piped up with: "Alright then, let's all go and start another kind of life, something more solitary like the hermits had." The suggestion could not have fallen on better ground. It was exactly what Teresa had been thinking about; just what she wanted. It was one of Teresa's most cherished convictions

that if quality was preferable to quantity in most things, it was paramount where religious persons were concerned. She was a firm believer in the efficacy of the select group. Few but committed. As she so incisively put it: "One person of quality will do more than many who are lacking in it" (WP.3,5). She believed too in the advantages of the small group; all know one another and communicate directly, and they are so few that it would be "brutal" not to love one another. The moment had come to tackle the task, to give wings to their restlessness and body to their ideas.

It was shortly after this that Teresa had a visit from Doña Guiomar de Ulloa, an intimate friend with whom she shared her troubles and her hopes. Half

Monastery of the Incarnation: interior of the church.

jokingly (and wholly in earnest) Teresa told her of her dreams of a little monastery. Far from taking it as a joke, Doña Guiomar became quite taken with the idea and promptly promised to provide the money for the venture.

Things moved quickly after that. Teresa consulted learned men and friends, and found everybody in agreement. The Carmelite Provincial, Fr. Angel de Salazar, was delighted to receive the proposed house under his obedience. The Jesuit confessor, Fr. Baltasar Alvarez, could see God's hand on the project. Fr. Pedro Ibáñez, a Dominican friar universally esteemed for learning and holiness, gave it his unreserved support. And that great ascetic, St. Peter of Alcántara, was more enthusiastic than anyone.

But the works of God — and this had all the signs of one — are never accomplished by a unanimous vote or along well-trodden paths. No sooner had word of the project got around the city than all hell broke loose (literally) on the principal people involved.

The Council of Avila, a city as proud of its noble lineage as it was short of money, refused even to consider the very idea of a monastery that would be supported by alms.

The nuns of the monastery of the Incarnation, Teresa's sisters, were affronted: she could serve God just as well here; there were lots of nuns that were holier than her; they needed money too. So the insults ran.

The preachers thundered and the ordinary people whispered against this nun who, under pretext of greater perfection, was surely up to no good.

Façade of St. Joseph's convent in Avila ("Las Madres").

It never rains but it pours. Now Doña Guiomar found she hadn't enough money to build the monastery, nor could she freely dispose of what she did have.

The Carmelite Provincial, fearful of worse to come, collapsed before the onslaught; not only did he withdraw his support for Teresa, but he sent her off to Toledo to comfort a noble widow. Her confessor told her to forget the whole thing.

There's a saying that a bench needs only three supports. Fortunately, the controversial foundress had three sterling supports: her own resolute determination; the loyalty of her closest friends; and, above and before all, her God. His was indubitably the leading role in this whole drama. The Lord left Teresa in no doubt about His will; powerfully, insistently He said: Yes, go ahead. As Teresa testifies: "His Majesty in-

sisted I strive for it with all my strength, and promised me it would be done... (He said) I was not to think that He was not being served in monasteries that were lax; that the world would be a sad place were it not for religious" (L.32,11).

When opposition intensified, the Lord was in control: "He told me not to weary myself... to do what my confessor told me by being silent for the time being" (L.33,3).

When she thought the house she bought was too small for a monastery, the Lord chided her: "I've told you to go on as best you can. Oh the greed of the human race to think you will lack land! How often have I slept beneath the skies for want of a place to go!" (L.33,12).

When she wasn't sure whether or not she should give

Bell of the first Teresian foundation, preserved in St. Joseph's in Avila.

"The Devil's Staircase," in St. Joseph's in Avila.

Interior of the church of St. Joseph's (Avila).

Courtyard of St. Joseph's.

"Our Lord with the beautiful eyes," in a hermitage (in the garden of St. Joseph's).

The Saint's cell at St. Joseph's (Avila). On the left, ledge on which St. Teresa wrote her "Life," "The Way of Perfection," "The Interior Castle"...

in on the question of income, Jesus set her straight: "On no account was she to neglect to make it poor" (L.35,6).

Later, when she had finally got the monastery founded, and people came shouting at the nuns in an effort to make them leave the place, the Lord said: "Don't you know I'm powerful; what are you afraid of?" He assured her that the work "would not be undone" (L.36,16).

But lest I weary the reader with quotations about the Lord's constant intervention, let us sum them all up in this last one where He assured Teresa "that this house was a paradise for His pleasure" (L.35,12).

We are still in 1561 and the first move has yet to be made. But with such comprehensive insurance, there was no holding Teresa. Besides, she could still count on those loyal friends, and she proceeded to organise them in a way that did her prowess at chess proud. To name only the more outstanding among them, they were Fathers Pedro Ibáñez, Baltasar Alvarez, Peter of Alcántara, whom we've already mentioned, Master Gaspar Daza, a holy layman called Francisco de Salcedo and her future standard bearer and chaplain Julian of Avila.

Since secrecy was of the essence, Teresa asked her brother-in-law Juan de Ovalle, who lived in Alba, to buy a house in Avila as if it were for himself, and to live in it while alterations were being carried out. That was in the summer of 1561.

Things began to come together quite rapidly now. Enough money for the project arrived from her brother Lorenzo in America. Teresa returned from Toledo where she had made some very good friends. The danger of being elected Prioress of the Incarnation appeared to have passed. And, finally, Gaspar Daza and Peter of Alcántara obtained the required permission from Rome and from Bishop Alvaro de Mendoza of Avila, for a monastery founded on alms. The latter also agreed that it should be directly subject to himself.

Primitive kitchen at St. Joseph's.

And so we come to the joyous and unforgettable day of 24 August 1862. Dawn had scarcely broken over the highest ramparts of the city walls when a shrill little bell, a bargain picked up in the course of preparations, woke the neighbourhood. Its message was simple: the first Discalced Carmelite monastery was no longer a project; it was a reality.

It was all very simple and modest. Gaspar Daza, representing the Bishop, gave the first four nuns their habits. Only close friends were present — those who had fought the good fight together.

That was by no means the end of the opposition, trials and tribulations which the nuns had come through. No indeed. But what was to follow had an effect similar to that of snow and ice on the grain of wheat; it helped the undertaking to sink in and take root.

As a contribution to this process, the City Council kept up a never-ending lawsuit over some alleged wells.

Mother Teresa was summoned back to the Incarnation, tried for her crime and threatened with monastic imprisonment. And, to make matters worse, word of these happenings was beginning to cause a stir at the courts of Madrid and Rome.

But in time the storm subsided and Teresa returned to her little dovecote, as she liked to call St. Joseph's, with her title to Foundress well and truly established. Since then St. Joseph's and everything in it speaks to us of St. Teresa. Every corner of the house bears the stamp of her spirit. Though we cannot see her we feel her presence. We cannot touch her, but we are continually touching objects she used, rooms she lived in. Near the monastery, deliberately small "so that it wouldn't make much noise when it fell on Judgement Day" (WP.2,9), and beside the church which was built at the beginning of the 17th century, is *St. Paul's Chapel.* God told Moses to remove his sandals, that the earth he walked on was holy. That is what one feels on entering this hallway to places hallowed by St. Teresa: the urge to strip ourselves of superfluities as the first Discalced nuns did before this altar.

The heart of the house is the Saint's *cell.* Sober, clean, with only a wooden bed for furniture and a cork mat for carpet. The typical environment of someone determined not to be held back by the things of this world, and whose only desire is to be "alone with Him alone". And there to the left, under that window which, according to Teresa, if she shut it she couldn't see and if she opened it she froze, is her magisterial podium. That rough stone seat was the desk on which, seated on the floor, she wrote her *Life* — that masterpiece similar to St. Augustine's *Confessions,* in which she sings of God's many mercies towards her. One might be pardoned for seeing in it the inaugural lecture of one who in time was destined to be declared a Doctor of the Church, and Mother of spiritual people.

We move on now to the *Chapter Room.* The outstanding feature her is her *Prioress's Seat,* her "other pulpit." No greater tribute can be paid her than to say that whatever difference there is between this seat and those used by the abbesses of her time was no coincidence; it was quite deliberate.

"Prioress's chair," the humble seat of the Saint's spiritual teaching.

The *Recreation Room* was another key place in Teresa's new style of monastic living. Naturally, it was based on friendship with God, on work, poverty and self-denial; but Teresa also brought to it that element of simple, friendly, cheerful and even humorous community relationships typical of one who had no time for "long-faced saints."

And let us not forget the *Kitchen,* a place where Teresa once gave the comforting reminder that God was as present "among the pots and pans" as He was anywhere else.

Just another step and we're in the *Garden;* at once the lungs and larder of the community, and their window to that little bit of clear Castilian sky — so transparent that they could sense God beyond.

On one side of the garden you have the *Samaritan's Well.* On the other, her famous *Hermitages:* humble

Statue of St. Joseph in the reredos of the main altar: St. Joseph's (Avila).

An image by Gregorio Hernández in the house where St. Teresa was born.

little buildings where great things were achieved as the Sisters, like the Fathers of the Desert, sought even greater retirement the better to immerse themselves in the Divinity.

There are so many interesting memories here that the list could go on endlessly: *the devil's staircase,* so called because he threw Teresa down them; pictures like that called *Christ of the Beautiful Eyes;* graves of some of the Saint's relatives and friends; the *mule chair* she once rode on; and so much more... Everything here speaks of her, but St. Joseph's is not the only place to do so.

It is unfortunate that these lines are intended only as a guide to places founded by St. Teresa; but it would be absurd to look only at her destinations and forget where she started from: the *Monastery of the Incarnation.*

Teresa knocked on its doors on 2nd November 1533. She had just been through a serious illness and looked upon entry here as building her tomb. It turned out instead to be the cradle of her virtues, the nursery from which several of her Discalced nuns were transplanted. The twenty-nine years she spent there left her with grateful and affectionate memories; surprising perhaps for a place she was eventually destined to leave in order to find her true vocation. The Incarnation is full of Teresian atmosphere: parlours, oratory, stairs, books, pictures and so many other objects tell us she has been there.

And the City itself? Its famous walls encase a veritable treasure chest, and the reader can admire these in the illustrations: *Carmen Gate, Our Lady of Charity, the house where St. Teresa was born, the convent of Our Lady of Grace,* and so many other places.

Castle of Arenas de San Pedro (Avila) seen by night. On the left, monument to St. Peter of Alcántara.

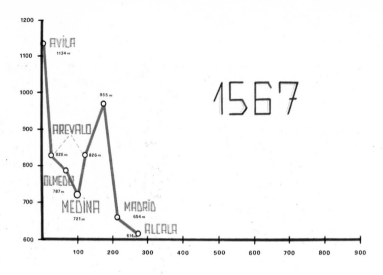

1567

Diagram of St. Teresa's travels in 1567 — the Foundation at Medina.

MEDINA

Teresian events and dates

— *August 1566: Fray Alonso Maldonado, missionary in America, fired the Saint with enthusiasm: millions of Indians had not heard the Gospel.*
— *February 1567: Juan Bautista Rubeo, the General of the Order, arrived in Avila and met the Saint at St. Joseph's.*
— *April 27th 1567: the Father General authorised Mother Teresa to found new carmels in Castile.*
— *June-July 1567: Mother Teresa requested the General's authorisation to found monasteries of Carmelite friars.*
— *Summer 1567: Fray John of the Cross, a student at Salamanca recently ordained as priest, went to Medina, where he said his first Mass.*
— *August 10th 1567: Juan Bautista Rubeo, the Father General, granted Mother Teresa powers to found two monasteries of Carmelite friars in Castile.*
— *August 13th 1567: the Saint set out from Avila, with a group of nuns, for Medina. They spent the night (13th-14th) at Arévalo.*
— *August 15th: Teresa inaugurated the carmel at Medina.*
— *August 16th: the Father General authorised her to found monasteries of Carmelite friars.*

Three episodes of contemporary history that bore on Mother Teresa's actions.

— *1566: Pius V, executor of the Tridentine Reform, was elected Sovereign Pontiff.*
— *1567 (April 16th): the Pope decided to undertake the reform of religious orders, and entrusted its execution to the bishops.*
— *1567 (September): the Diuke of Alba reached Flanders, where he established the tribunal "des troubles."*

"Book of the Foundations," beginning of the autograph relating the foundation of Medina: "Chapter III: how plans began to be made for the foundation of the convent of St. Joseph's in Medina del Campo."

Exterior of the Medina convent. Drawing by the Belgian architect Hye Hoys (1866).

MEDINA DEL CAMPO (VALLADOLID) ST. JOSEPH'S MONASTERY 15.8.1567

Once the storms that surrounded the early days of St. Joseph's, Avila, had passed, it was a little haven of peace and grace; reminiscent of those calm lakes which, surrounded by steep mountains, are not troubled by even the slightest breeze and reflect the heavens above them with absolute clarity. For Teresa the next five years, during which she was prioress, were "the most restful in her life" (F.1,1). With the thirteen nuns, which was the most she would take at that time (she allowed twenty-one later), "she was enjoying herself with people who were so holy and pure that their only thought was for the praise and service of God" (F.1,2).

But pleasures, however pure, were not this woman's staff of life. Teresa could no more contain the volcanic expansion of love within her than we could hold air in our fist. One day a Franciscan missionary,

Side view of the Castle of "La Mota" (Medina).

Alonso de Maldonado, happened to visit the community and proceeded to horrify the sisters with his tales of the multitude of souls being lost in the Americas, or the Indies, as they called them then.

Shortly afterwards came the first, and unexpected, visit from the Carmelite Prior General, Fr. Rubeo. A dreaded visit, perhaps, because he could have been angry with Teresa for leaving the Incarnation and transferring her obedience to the bishop. Instead, what he saw there so thrilled him that he gave her freedom to make further foundations.

To be able to found, to want to do so in order that through prayer fewer souls would be lost, and to look out for her next conquest could be said to be all one

Overall view of Arévalo, on the way from Avila to Medina.

Interior of the Carmelite convent.

Convent of Medina, interior courtyard.

Hermitage of Mount Carmel. Garden of the convent.

thing in Teresa's mind. And the place she thought of was Medina del Campo.

There were various reasons for this choice: it was near — two days' ride on a mule. She knew an influential man there, who was ready to help: Fr. Baltasar Alvarez, the Jesuit rector and her one-time confessor. The Carmelite prior, Fr. Antonio de Heredia, was also well-disposed and knew a lady who would sell them a house. Besides, Medina itself was quite a cosmopolitan commercial centre, well-known both in Europe and the Americas; it had a touch of universality.

This latter aspect, however, was also a complicating factor. A proud city that engraved a motto like "No office for the King; no benefice for the Pope" on its coat of arms was unlikely to welcome such a foundation. But Teresa's friends got to work; the clergy, nobility and city fathers gave unanimous approval. All was arranged; Mother Teresa was informed that she could come whenever she liked.

No sooner said than done. With a little borrowed money for capital, "two nuns from St. Joseph's and myself, with four from the Incarnation, left Avila... with our chaplain, Fr. Julián de Avila" (F.3,2). This was their first founding expedition and it had an air of adventure, exploration, and conquest about it. Notwithstanding much advice to the contrary, the little party set off in the full light of day, as if to put the humiliations suffered on the occasion of their taking possession of St. Joseph's behind them for good.

That was 13th August 1567. They passed through Cardeñosa and Gotarrendura, full of childhood memories for Teresa, and stopped at Arévalo to spend the night with "some devout ladies" (F.3,2). Either the devil had been sleeping and now suddenly woke up, or God doesn't allow His works to be accomplished without contradiction. Whichever way you look at it, contradiction lay in wait.

Word came from Medina that the Augustinians had raised objections to the house they had rented. The

Altar vestments embroidered by Saint Teresa.

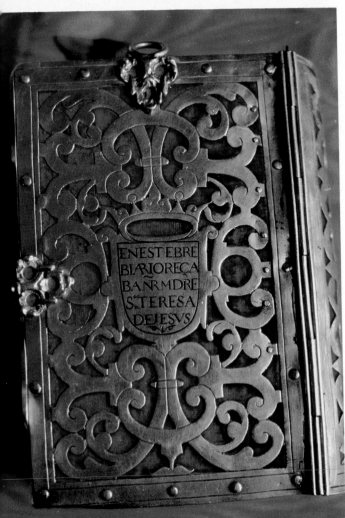

Breviary used by Mother Teresa, now bound with a silver cover.

nuns, already in Arévalo, were instructed not to leave Avila! How they felt is well summed up in these lines of the faithful Fr. Julián: ''When I heard this and remembered the fanfare with which we left Avila, I thought of the laughter and mockery that would greet our return... It upset me quite a lot.''

The night was spent planning and making decisions rather than sleeping. The final decision was to go on to Medina and stay in the house that Fr. Antonio had been trying to buy, no matter what state it was in.

So after a detour to visit the bishop of Avila at Olmedo, the party reached Medina after nightfall. They stopped at the Carmelite Priory, and decided to go the rest of the way on foot so as not to attract attention. Only they forgot that that was the night when the bulls were being penned for the following day's bullfight!

Let us hear Julián de Avila on the incident! ''We took the vestments and other things necessary for saying Mass (from the Carmelite Priory) and, without more ado, set off on foot — nuns, clergy, the prior and two or three friars — taking a roundabout way to avoid the bulls, which were being penned just then... We were all well-laden and looked like a party of gypsies who had just robbed a church. Certainly, if we had met any police they would have had to take us to jail until they found out where priests, friars and nuns were going at that hour of the night.''

They eventually reached the house, armed with a letter from its owner requesting the caretaker to assist them. But what a night lay in store for them! When the caretaker and his wife had been roused, they insisted on summoning a notary to record all the events of the night. Meanwhile, Teresa and her friends cleared a hallway of rubbish, cleaned it up and decorated the crumbling walls with a few hangings. At last an altar was ready, someone rang a bell, the Carmelite prior said Mass, and the Blessed Sacrament was reserved.

Teresa was delighted with herself; "To see another church where the Blessed Sacrament was reserved was always one of my greatest comforts," she said (F. 3,10). That was fine in the dark, but when the full light of the Castilian sun on 15th August showed up the real situation her joy over one tabernacle more became acute anxiety that she might soon have one tabernacle less.

Her delight, then, was short-lived, "because after Mass I looked out of the window at the inner court-yard only to find that the walls had actually fallen in places... When I realised that His Majesty had been placed on the side of the street in the dangerous times we live in because of those Lutherans, how my heart was troubled!" (F. 3,10).

Nevertheless, there they had to stay for another week, when a merchant offered Teresa the upper storey of his house until her own was fit to live in. That took another two months. Later, through the generosity of Doña Elena de Quiroga (who became a nun herself in 1581), a pretty little church was added to the building, thus completing the foundation.

There are still a few points we would like to touch on in this hurried account of the Medina foundation.

The first is to fill the reader in a little on that devotion to the Eucharist we saw evidence of in Teresa's enthusiasm over one more tabernacle. She actually placed a watch on it every night, and even got up to check than the watchmen were awake.

Like every believer, Teresa was aware that the God we worship is one who likes to communicate with us. But she also knew that He tends to disguise this communication — in a burning bush, in wind, in MAN. She was in love with God made man, but was aware that since the Ascension He could be found only in the tabernacle. "The Lord had given her such strong faith that when she heard people saying they would like to have been alive when Jesus was on earth, she used to laugh to herself because she regarded Him as

Monument to St. John of the Cross at Fontiveros (Avila).

being just as much present in the Blessed Sacrament as He had been then; so what difference did it make to them?" (WP. 34,6).

Perhaps that is why she received her greatest graces after Communion, and why she insisted with her daughters: "Stay with Him willingly. Don't lose so good an opportunity for your business with Him as the time after Communion affords you" (WP. 34,12).

A point that cannot be overlooked when speaking of Medina is that this was where Teresa first met Fr John of the Cross, the man destined to be the first Discalced Carmelite friar, a saint, mystical poet and Doctor of the Church.

Teresa had often thought about how good it would be if her Order also had a male branch to minister to the spiritual needs of her nuns. After getting permission for this and discussing it with Fr Antonio de Heredia, who to her surprise offered to be the first, one day "a young Father happened to come there... whose name was Fr John of the Cross. I praised the Lord and, having spoken with him, was very pleased with him. He told me that he too (like Fr Antonio) wanted to go and join the Carthusians. I explained what I had in mind and pressed him to wait until the Lord gave us a monastery. I emphasised how good it would be if he could perfect himself in his own Order... He promised to wait, provided he didn't have to wait too long" (F. 3,17). He didn't have long to wait, but we'll return to that later.

Here then is the Medina Carmel, snug in the shadow of the Castillo de la Mota, a castle which would seem to defend the footsteps of St. Teresa against the shifting sands of time. You can see such signs of her presence here as her *Breviary,* the *embroidery* with which she illustrated Biblical passages in gold and silver on vestments, her *account book,* objects and places in the monastery that are particularly associated with her. Yet these things are but a shadow of the most precious thing she left behind: her spirit is as much alive there today as when she sat in this convent writing her *Book of Foundations.*

Altarpiece in the church at Fontiveros.

Baptismal font of St. John of the Cross (Fontiveros -Avila).

Sa pitulo / x trata de como Salio de medina del campo para la fundacion de Sa Josef de malago

"Book of the Foundations," which narrates the beginning of the journey to Malagón: "Chapter IX: tells how she left Medina del Campo for the foundation of St. Joseph's at Malagón."

Malagón (Ciudad Real).

MALAGON

Dates and occurrences relating to Teresa's third foundation

— *January-February 1568: Teresa travelled from Medina del Campo to Alcalá de Henares. She advised María de Jesús and put in order the carmel founded in Alcalá by the latter. The Saint passed through Madrid.*
— *March: the Saint left Alcalá and reached Toledo. In Doña Luisa de la Cerda's mansion she signed (March 30th) the documents for the foundation of her third carmel: Malagón.*
— *March 31st: Mother Teresa set out for Malagón. The little house with the new carmel was inaugurated on April 11th.*
— *April: Teresa confided the manuscript of the book of her Life to Doña Luisa de la Cerda, for the latter to deliver to St. John of Avila in Montilla (Córdoba).*
— *May-June: a series of letters (at least four) to the bearer of the manuscript, exhorting her to keep her promise to deliver it to St. John of Avila. The Saint was to leave Malagón without any reassuring news.*
— *May 19th: Teresa left Malagón for Avila, where she spent almost all the month of June.*
— *June 30th: a further journey, from Avila to Medina. On the way she visited the farm at Duruelo, later to be St. John of the Cross's monastery.*
— *July 1st: at Medina, the inner voice urged her to found the Valladolid carmel.*
— *July 6th: Fray John of the Cross bore letters to Avila to negotiate the Duruelo foundation.*
— *August 9th: accompanied by Fray John of the Cross, the Saint set out from Medina for Valladolid.*
— *September 12th: St. John of Avila wrote to Mother Teresa expressing approval of the book of her Life.*
— *May 10th 1569: St. John of Avila died at Montilla.*

An important development: *the approval of Teresa's first book by the great Master of spirituals, John of Avila. This book was for its authoress no more nor less than "her soul"; and it contained an enormous effort to bring light to the abyss of her life. The letter from the "Apostle of Andalusia" resolved the accumulation of anxiety and doubt that had troubled her for years. It was the voice of the Church corroborating her prophetic charisma, her vocation as a writer, and her experience of God.*

External view of the convent at Malagón; drawing by Hye Hoys (1866-1867).

MALAGON (CIUDAD REAL)
ST. JOSEPH'S MONASTERY
11.4.1568

The events described in the last chapter have brought us up to about October 1567. Mother Teresa of Jesus is comforted and praising the Lord that her Medina nuns "are following in the footsteps of those at St Joseph's, Avila" (F. 9,1).

Meanwhile, in Toledo, her great friend Doña Luisa de la Cerda, the Duke of Medinaceli's sister, and in fact the person Teresa had been sent to console on the death of her husband, had found out something which was about to give Teresa another change of scene. She had found out about the permission Teresa had to make further foundations, and thought it would be a good idea to get her to found a monastery in honour of her late husband in the city of which he had been lord —Malagón.

Windmills, landscape of La Mancha.

Church of Saint Mary Major, at Daimiel.

Referring to this lady, Teresa wrote: "She began to pester me... I wanted none of it, because the place was so small that some sort of endowment would have to be arranged and that was something to which I was very much opposed... I discussed it with learned men and with my confessor, and they told me I was wrong. The Council (of Trent) had permitted this, they said, and a monastery in which the Lord could be served so well should not be dropped in favour of my opinion. With this and the lady's continuing insistence I had no choice but to give in. She gave an adequate endowment, because I like the monasteries to be either completely poor or so provided for that the nuns do not have to pester anybody for what they need" (F. 9, 2-3).

So Teresa is about to take another lesson in that difficult course from which she would graduate with the title "God's wandering lady." Accompanied by Ana de los Angeles, who was to be prioress of the new community, she set out from Medina. A stop-over at St. Joseph's, Avila, to collect another nun for the undertaking, was a joy for all concerned. It was Teresa's first return to the monastery which she thought of as "hers" in a special way. But the journey ahead was long, so the visit had to be cut short. The first stage took them over the mountains. Then a fortnight's rest at the home of Doña Leonor de Mascareñas, one-time governess to King Philip II, in Madrid, and on once more towards Alcalá.

They entered the city by the Madrid Gate and stopped a little way in on the right-hand side. Here a difficult task awaited the Foundress: she had to temper the rigorous observance of a community which the Ven. María de Jesús had founded there, much on the same

Malagón, monument to the Saint.

Niche with the Saint's "ledge," opposite the convent at Malagón.

lines as Avila and Medina. Teresa had met this Andalusian widow, who had journeyed barefoot to Rome to obtain permission to found her Discalced Carmelite monastery, at Doña Luisa's palace in Toledo. Since their objectives were similar, they had a lot to talk about and quickly became friends. And, according to St. Teresa, it was this woman who could neither read nor write who taught her "what with all her reading of the constitutions" she had not noticed, namely: that the Rule she was seeking to reform forbade property and endowments. This was a detail that strongly influenced the style of Teresa's reform and caused her no few headaches along the way.

It was now Teresa's turn to return the favour. At the foundress's own request, she proceeded to remove from this monastery everything that had turned it into an arena of mortification, or a hairshirt market, and to turn it into one of the simplest and most cheerful of her dovecotes.

That took her two months, and then it was on to Toledo, where they stayed with Doña Luisa in her palace overlooking the city. It was her first visit since the days when preparations for Avila were afoot; so memories came flooding back. Memories of God, for it was here that she had written her *Life;* memories of the attentions of that noble lady; memories of her conversations with the servants, from whose midst she won that sterling vocation, María de San José (Salazar). Here she could reminisce and finalise the details of the foundation on which she had embarked. That done, and having summoned four more nuns from the Incarnation at Avila, Teresa set out for Malagón. She was accompanied by Doña Luisa, with some of her servants, and a ponderous Jesuit,

Gallery of the interior courtyard of the convent.

Interior courtyard — convent of Malagón.

mischievously nicknamed "the eternal father" by Teresa. Fifteen leagues lay ahead; rough, sometimes mountainous, country, but traversed with rather less difficulty than expected, owing to Doña Luisa's knowledge of the countryside. Finally, on 1st April, they arrived, and in no time had every able-bodied person in the village organised to help them. As usual, the house was not yet ready for occupation, so they stayed in Doña Luisa's imposing castle for the time being.

On 11th April, "Palm Sunday, a procession of townsfolk came to fetch us, and, with lowered veils and white mantles, we proceeded to the parish church. There a sermon was preached and then the Blessed Sacrament was borne to our monastery" (F. 9,5).

Before long they learned that it had been a mistake to choose a house so close to the market. Mother Teresa was immediately allowed to choose a better site, and even offered one at the north end of the town. This she refused in favour of one on the south side, saying it was destined for a Franciscan monastery. And she proved to be right: some time afterwards the sons of her protector, St. Peter of Alcántara, came to settle there. According to tradition, Teresa saw a singularly white dove perched on an olive tree south of the town, and chose that site for her definitive foundation there.

Doña Luisa allowed Teresa complete freedom in the design, building and furnishing of this monastery. The original accounts and other documentation concerning it are still in the convent safe to prove it. Work began immediately, but it was eleven years before she could return for the solemn transfer from old monastery to new. She may of course have visited it

Statue of St. Teresa in her cell.

Statue of St. Teresa, convent of Malagón.

in the meantime, while on one of her journeys, for she certainly used nuns from there in subsequent foundations.

Her arrival in Malagón on 25th November 1579 is thus described by her companion, Anne of St. Bartholomew: "After a dreadful journey and several bad nights, she arrived so ill that every bone in her body ached and she was unfit to leave her bed." But a woman of Teresa's energy is difficult to keep in bed. As soon as the builders reported that the work would take about another six months, she was up at dawn the following day to see for herself. She inspected what had been done, made her calculations regarding the remainder, and announced that it was to be ready for the Feast of the Immaculate Conception — just twelve days away!

Leaving masons and friends to recover from that shock as best they could, she went on site from morning till night — skipping prayer times, meals and rest — and, when she was not lending a hand herself, she directed operations from a stone "podium" which is still preserved to this day. Needless to say, the builders met her deadline!

We cannot end our account of this foundation without mentioning some of the features which distinguished it from the rest.

In the first place, it was the only monastery which the Foundress herself built from scratch. Elsewhere, conditions about the place, shortage of money, or the adaptation of buildings all had a restricting influence. This building expresses fully what Teresa thought was suitable for her nuns — the kind of building, the lay-out, the space required.

For that reason St. Joseph's at Malagón is a real relic, and the nuns go to great pains to keep it absolutely

Original revolving window (Malagón).

unchanged. Even maintenance is carried out with the original materials. No wonder "the plans" have been requested from all over the world for new Carmels.

Another point about this third foundation is the way it illustrates the astounding flexibility of spirit which enabled Teresa to adapt her ideal of a Reformed Carmel to varying circumstances.

We sometimes take as "fidelity to the spirit, to the primitive ideal or charisma" what in reality is only spiritual narrowness, inertia, or simply the convenient repetition of rules — something that is much easier to do than to constantly adapt them to the needs of the moment.

When she was founding St. Joseph's, Avila, Teresa defended tooth and nail her ideal — based on the primitive rule — of a radically poor house, without money or endowment. Yet, here she accepts the latter for the reasons we have mentioned.

She also agreed to go ahead with this foundation notwithstanding the difficulty which the nuns would have in finding fish in this Castilian hinterland, thus making it difficult to observe abstinence from meat, which seemed such an important point of the Rule.

And then there was the contemplative life itself: to be "alone with God alone" was "the reason the Lord had brought them together there." But when Teresa

Communion grille.

Water filter.

realised the grave social needs of the townspeople, she had her nuns finance a sewing workshop for the girls and paid a priest and an assistant to teach the boys. "What other alms but this can we give?" she said.

Finally, another new, though not original, element: it was here that she first admitted "lay sisters." These were nuns who undertook the manual work in the house; they had no choral obligations themselves and greatly facilitated the heavy liturgical commitment of the rest of the community.

Let no one think, however, that such modifications here and in some subsequent foundations rendered them in any way inferior. No, indeed. And lest such an idea should occur to anyone, including Teresa, Jesus himself assured her "that He would be well served in that house" (F. 9,5).

A last point. To honour the people who first made this Carmel possible and who have so lovingly supported it to this day, let us state one simple fact: if Teresa of Jesus is the Saint of a place called Avila, Malagón is undoubtedly the place of a Saint called Teresa of Jesus.

The love of the people of Malagón for St. Teresa and her daughters is proverbial. And the shrine in the little square leading to the monastery and church is a symbol of it. There, framed for posterity, is a likeness of the Saint and the famous stone on which she used to rest while directing the building work. The townsfolk testify to their devotion with a perpetually burning oil lamp, plenty of electric lights all the year round, and an abundance of fresh flowers. They never pass their little shrine without making some sign of faith and devotion.

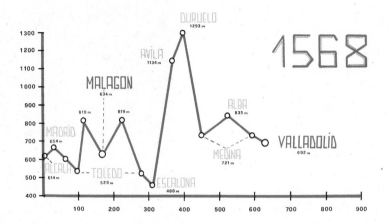

Sketch of the journey to the foundations of Malagón and Valladodid.

Autograph of the "Book of the Foundations: beginning of the foundation of the convent at Duruelo: "Chapter XIII: tells how and by whom the first convent of the primitive Rule was founded for friars, in MDLXVIII. — Before I went to this foundation in Valladolid, as had already been arranged with Padre Antonio..."

VALLADOLID

St. Teresa's route from Toledo to Valladolid 1568

— late May 1568: the Saint left Toledo for Escalona.
— June 2nd: she arrived in Avila, and paused there until the end of the month.
— June 30th: she set out from Avila towards Medina. St. Teresa made a detour so as to visit the farm at Duruelo.
— July 1st: at Medina del Campo.
— August 10th: the Saint arrived in Valladolid. She had travalled from Medina with Fr. John of the Cross.
— August 15th: the new carmel was established at Río de Olmos, on the banks of the Pisuerga.
— September 30th: St. Teresa took her leave of Fr. John of the Cross, who set off for Duruelo.
— November 28th 1568: Fr. John of the Cross and Fr. Antonio Heredia set up the new Carmelite monastery at the little house in Duruelo.

An important event: Fr. John of the Cross's indoctrination by Mother Teresa. She was 53 years old, he 26. Fr. John was willingly trained in the "style of life, brotherhood in the group. The two were profoundly different; but they shared the mystic vocation and the depth of their experience of God.

Exterior of the convent, Valladolid. Drawing by Hye Hoys (1866-1867).

VALLADOLID
MONASTERY OF THE CONCEPTION OF OUR LADY OF MOUNT CARMEL
15.8.1568

St Teresa tells the story of this foundation in ch. 10 of her *Book of Foundations*. This is how she begins:

"Four or five months before I founded the Malagón monastery, I was talking to an important gentleman (she is referring to D. Bernardino de Mendoza, the bishop of Avila's brother) and he told me that if I wanted to make a foundation in Valladolid, he would give a house he had there, with a fine big garden. Though I was not very keen on it as a place for a foundation, because it was almost a quarter of a league from the town, I accepted...

Two months later, this young man was laid low by a sudden illness which deprived him of the power of speech. He could scarcely make his confession, though he did make many signs to indicate that he

Valladolid. Cloister of the National Sculpture Museum.

was asking God's forgiveness. Shortly afterwards he died. The Lord told me that his salvation had been very much at risk, but that He had had mercy on him because of the favour he did His Mother in giving that house as a monastery of her Order. He would not leave Purgatory, however, until the first Mass had been said in that house. I was so conscious of the grave sufferings of that soul that, though I wanted to found in Toledo, I left that aside for the moment and tried to found as quickly as possible in Valladolid instead."

We can measure Teresa's haste on the calendar. Having made provisional arrangements for her nuns, she left Malagón on 19th May 1568. On 29th May she left Toledo for Escalona and spent June in Avila, where she arrived "rather tired." She was still prioress of Avila and could not leave it as quickly as she might have liked to; the absence just past and that which she was preparing for meant that a lot of details had to be attended to so that the community could carry on without her.

Setting out again on June 30th, she reached Medina after losing a lost of time looking for a little place called Duruelo, of which more later. Here another delay for community business and matters relating to her desire, fast becoming an obsession, to found a house of Discalced Carmelite friars. In the midst of her preoccupation with this dream the Lord gave her a reminder about Valladolid: "While I was praying one day, He told me to hurry: that that soul was suffering a lot" (F. 10,3).

So it was back on the road again, and quickly to her destination — Río Olmos, a mile and a half or so from Valladolid. With her were three nuns from Avila, three from Medina, a postulant and Fr John of the Cross. The man who was to be her first Discalced friar was having his first outing with his sisters and chatting with them about God and the new lifestyle he was to copy from them.

"As soon as I saw the house I was quite distressed, because I realised that it would be foolish to expect nuns to live there. The beautiful garden made it very pleasant, but it couldn't be healthy so near the river" (F. 10,3). Nevertheless, she quickly got on with the necessary adjustments. Everything was done with the utmost secrecy, for her faithful chaplain, Fr Julián, had not yet obtained the permission of the ecclesiastical authorities for the foundation.

In the midst of all this who should pay them an unexpected visit but the Vicar General of the City. He must have been impressed, because he immediately allowed them to say Mass and promised to expedite the permission they were looking for.

"Little did I think that what had been said to me about that gentleman would be fulfilled just then... But when the priest approached us with the Host at Communion time, just as I was about to receive it I had a vision of the said gentleman beside the priest, his face resplendent and full of joy... He thanked me for what I had done to enable him to leave Purgatory and go to Heaven" (F. 10,5).

The official opening took place that same week: 15th August, Feast of the Assumption.

It was not long before St. Teresa's misgivings about the healthiness of the place began to be justified.

Front courtyard of the convent, Valladolid.

Autograph of the "Way of Perfection" in a silver case, and a facsimile reproduction of the same.

Hermitage of St. Teresa, in the garden of the convent.

Beautiful though its situation was, standing between the Pisuerga and Olmos rivers, always fresh and green behind screens of poplar trees, it was nevertheless extremely damp and unhealthy. Soon, all the sisters had been laid low by malaria. As long as she could stay on her feet Mother Teresa served and fed them all, made their beds and nursed them. It became only too obvious that they would have to move elsewhere.

Doña María de Mendoza, a sister both of their late benefactor and of the bishop of Avila, undertook to find them another site. The agreement was that in return for Río Olmos she would find them a place on the outskirts of the city, near the main road leading from St. Clare's Gate. The property she had in mind, however, belonged to an entailed estate, and negotiations for its purchase were slow. Meanwhile, the big-hearted Doña María removed the community to her own house, where "she killed them with kindness," and there they spent Christmas. It was there that on Christmas Eve St. Teresa "gave a talk the like of which they had never heard before." According to the chronicler of this event, "She spoke of the Infant's tears, the Mother's poverty, the hardness of the crib, the severity of the weather and the uncomfortableness of the stable. Such was the spirit and fervour with which she spoke that everyone went away comforted and happy; ready and willing to face the challenge of any hardship."

The new monastery was eventually ready for occupation on February 3rd, the Feast of St, Blaise. The Bishop of Avila attended with all the clergy of the city, both secular and regular. Nobility and grandees turned out in force. The streets were bedecked with bunting; lights and perfumed candles burned along the way. Quite a procession, by all accounts. And all eyes were on Mother Teresa, who by now was beginning to be looked upon as a saint.

So much for the facts of the foundation; but there are some other things worth mentioning here too.

First of all, the community. Doña María de Ocampo,

that niece of Teresa's who first suggested reforming the Carmelite life in one of their little get-togethers at the Incarnation, became Sister María Bautista and prioress of this monastery. Here, too, lived Casilda de Padilla, the nun who so impressed Teresa that she devoted nearly two chapters of the *Book of Foundations* to a moving account of her exemplary life, so that the memory of it should never die.

In fact, in the 16th and 17th centuries this monastery produced a whole generation of humanist nuns. They read Latin, Greek and Hebrew; they were well-versed in the Scriptures; and many were noteworthy poets, especially Cecilia del Nacimiento who could stand comparison with Lope de Vega or Quevedo.

This monastery is also the proud repository of some of St. Teresa's writings. St. Teresa wrote her *Way of Perfection* twice; the second version is in this monastery. The community treasures with equal love the greatest single holding of her letters — over fifty in all. Looking at them, one cannot help thinking how much greater St. Teresa's literary and doctrinal legacy would be if only all the communities of friars and nuns had been as careful to keep all her letters as this one was.

The last point we would like to consider brings us back to the beginning of this account of the Valladolid foundation. We mentioned the detour which St. Teresa's party made in search of a little place called Duruelo, a place she was to visit again on her way to Toledo. What, you might ask, was the attraction of such an out of the way little village? It was here that Teresa's dream of extending her Reform to the Carmelite friars had just come true. When speaking of the Medina foundation, we mentioned the agreement which Teresa made with Frs Antonio de Heredia and John of the Cross (or John of St. Matthias as he then was) — her promise not to keep them waiting. The best she could do in the short term was to accept the offer of a tumbledown shack in Duruelo from a certain Don Rafael of Avila. After laborious negotiations she obtained the permission of the male branch of the

Carmelite Order for a new expression of their life. It was begun in Duruelo on 28th November 1568 by the two fathers mentioned above, and they became henceforth Frs Antony of Jesus and John of the Cross.

Speaking of the extreme poverty of this house, Teresa wrote: ''It didn't take long to get the house ready because, although they would have liked to do

Statue of St. Teresa by a pupil of Gregorio Fernández.

Garden of the convent.

Hazel tree planted by the Saint. Garden of the convent, Valladolid.

more, there just wasn't any money." She was deeply moved by what she saw: "I shall never forget a little wooden cross they had over the holy water font. It had a little paper picture of Christ stuck to it, and I found it more devotional than if it had been really well made" (F. 14,2 & 7).

What did Teresa expect of her Discalced friars? Surely, to maintain and communicate all she had discovered and experienced herself. What Teresa had discovered was a new image of the Almighty Father. She saw him as a friend, embroiled in the affairs of men, so near that He dwelt among the pots and pans, or hid within the castle of each person's soul, so easily approachable that she described prayer as the conversation of friends.

In Christ, Teresa discovered the Master, the living Book, God pre-fabricated to the measure of her woman's heart, the Spouse whose honour is hers just as hers is His.

Teresa discovered the Church in all the glory of its dignity as Bride of Christ, but nevertheless, "beset by great evils." She did not clamour against hierarchies or faulty structures; she was content to be a faithful and obedient daughter, and to see to it that her daughters at least would be the same. In this fight she found a powerful and definitive weapon: for the good of the Church she created a new style of monastic life — communities which would be "little colleges of Christ." She saw them as select groups which, because of their small numbers, the poverty with which they surrounded themselves, their thirst for depth, the simplicity of their ways, their contagious cheerfulness, and constant prayer for the defenders of the Church, would be the light, the salt and the leaven that the world needed.

Antique statue of Our Lady in alabaster, venerated in the convent of Valladolid.

She was, as she well knew, only a weak and worthless woman. For that reason she needed a male branch. These men, with their experience of God, their learning, and a knowledge of the nuns' lifestyle, would make the Reformed Carmel complete. They would teach, encourage, and watch over them. Besides, being men, they could and would sally forth to the foreign missions to prevent so many souls from being lost.

God rewarded her with a very rare gift: the personification of all her dreams in the humble person of the first Discalced Carmelite friar, Fr John of the Cross. When she spoke with him through the parlour grills in Medina and Valladolid, taught him her ways and made his first habit for him, she found him to be a refined, open and learned man in search of a very specific vocation... That won her heart completely.

John of the Cross was a prayerful man and a lover of solitude. He could capture beauty in poetry with the best. He loved his Order. But, above all, he was open to the new "brotherly" style of life created by Teresa, and had no hangups about learning it from a group of women who were already living it.

The chief thing that made Teresa so enthusiastic about John of the Cross, however, was his experience of God. Rarely in history have two people met who were so immersed in the mystery of God, so capable of savouring it, of expressing it in poetry and prose and, above all, of spreading it about them.

John of the Cross was the embodiment of all the teaching, advice and guidelines which Teresa imparted to the friars. Because of what she gave them through him and because of what she suffered that they might see the light of day, they have always regarded her as their Foundress.

[handwritten facsimile text]

"Book of the Foundations," beginning of the foundation of the Carmelite convent in Toledo: "Chapter XV: tells about the foundation of the convent of St. Joseph in the city of Toledo, MDLXIX."

Toledo.

TOLEDO

St. Teresa's route
from Valladolid to Toledo
1569

— *December 1568: from Valladolid she arranged the foundation of the carmel at Toledo: exchange of letters with Father Pablo Hernández and the founders.*
— *February 22nd 1569: Teresa began the jouney from Valladolid to Medina and Duruelo. Interlude of two weeks at St. Joseph's, Avila.*
— *March 24th: Teresa arrived in Toledo. Problems. The ecclesiastical governor's authorisation to found was not forthcoming until May 8th.*
— *May 14th: the Saint established the Toledo carmel, her fifth foundation — her quinta ("fifth" and "villa") of rest.*
— *May 30th: further travels — from Toledo to Pastrana, via the Court.*

Important: *Mother Teresa already knew Toledo. She knew the city's imperial splendour, its palaces and nobility. Now she got a first-hand view of the tragedy of the primate church. Its archbishop, the Dominican Bartolomé de Carranza — a very spiritual man, a good writer, friend of Father Granada, and also probably a kindred soul of Mother Teresa — had been in various prisons since 1559. Toledo's Church meanwhile underwent the consequences. The Saint was to have a personal confrontation with the ecclesiastical governor, Don Gómez Tello de Girón.*

Exterior of the Carmelite convent, Toledo, drawing by Hye Hoys (1866-1867).

TOLEDO
ST. JOSEPH'S MONASTERY
14.5.1569

Let's take a walk through the Jewish quarter of Toledo. It is May 14th 1569 and in a little while the sun will be quite strong. But just now it is only half light, enough to see the warren of short, narrow, winding streets which seem deliberately designed to hide the famous arabesque synagogue.

Down below, the river Tagus makes one last bend, as if waving farewell on its way to Extremadura. But up here near the synagogue, in a low, cramped little house, Mother Teresa has just inaugurated her fifth monastery of Discalced Carmelite nuns. The story of that foundation is what we are now about to relate. Let Teresa herself start it: ''In the city of Toledo there lived an honourable man, a servant of God, who was a merchant. This man never married. He lived a very devout life, and was very truthful and upright. He

conducted his business honestly and amassed wealth only in order to put it to some use that would be pleasing to God. But he became mortally ill. His name was Martín Ramírez'' (F. 15,1).

A Jesuit priest called Pablo Hernández (one of those who accompanied Teresa to Malagón) knew this man and his intentions. He went to see him, and suggested that a monastery of Discalced Carmelite nuns would fit the bill admirably. The dying man agreed, but left the matter in the hands of his brother, Alonso Alvarez. At which juncture ''God took him to Himself.''

When Teresa was in Malagón, therefore, she knew of this possibility, and looked forward to making a foundation in the imperial city of Toledo for a variety of reasons. As we have seen, she had a reason to found first in Valladolid and was unable to leave there until near the end of February. From Valladolid she went to Medina, where she decided definitively on the kind of enclosure which her monasteries were to have. From there she visited Duruelo, and was amazed to find the once dignified Fr Anthony sweeping the porch; he proclaimed by word and deed that he had swept away the dust of honour and vainglory. A short stop at her beloved St. Joseph's, Avila, to keep in contact with her loved ones there, and she was finally on the road for Toledo.

They travelled those twenty leagues, to quote Isabel de Santo Domingo, who was not used to such journeys, ''with great propriety, veils down so as not to be seen, and observing our times for mental and vocal prayer.'' At Tiemblo they stayed the night, and almost experienced the sword of an angry guest whose room they had taken by mistake. Then on through Cadarso de los Vidrios, with its reformed Franciscans so dear to Teresa's heart. After a last stop at San Martín de Valdeiglesias, noted for its fine pines, good wine, and the fortress of the Duque del

Entrance to the church of St. Clement (Toledo).

Choir of St. Clement's (Toledo).

Infantado, they reached Toledo on 24 March, the vigil of the Annunciation.

Toledo still retained something of the sparkle of its former splendour. Encircled by three walls, its centre still housed enough nobility to cause contemporary chroniclers to refer to it as "the head of the kingdom and the heart of Spain."

The population of the city has been calculated at about 90,000, but they were not as united or as homogeneous as the confining grip of the Tagus might lead us to think. The social stratification, which ranged from showy opulence to the direst poverty, made its presence felt everywhere, even in monasteries, sodalities, parishes and suchlike. These differences, with their accompanying envy and sensitiveness on matters of honour, were to have a disturbing effect on the new Carmel too. But now we anticipate; let us return to the subjects of our story.

The three nuns from Avila entered by the Cambrón Gate and alighted before the welcoming palace of their friend Doña Luisa de la Cerda. With such connections, with the late Martín Ramírez's money a certainty, with the King's permission only a formality, there was little to worry about. All they really lacked was the Archbishop's permission.

A long time ago the Lord said through the mouth of His prophet: "My thoughts are not your thoughts," a sentiment echoed by the proverb "Man proposes, but God disposes." Soon, Teresa would be heard repeating frequently that "God's ways are not our ways."

Teresa immediately set about obtaining ecclesiastical permission. At the time, Archbishop Carranza was a prisoner of the Inquisition in Valladolid, and nobody (including Doña Luisa) had been able to get anything from the cathedral chapter or from the archbishop's deputy. Their argument was that Toledo already had 1,200 nuns and that they were consequently not allowing any more convents to be founded. That

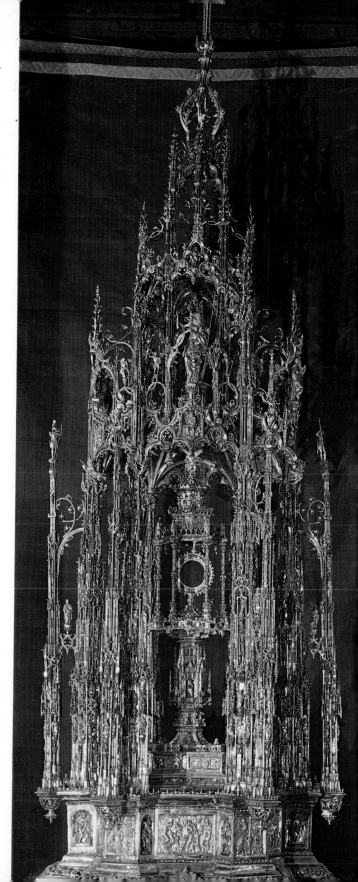

sounds quite reasonable, but it was really only a blind. The real reason had more to do with the enmity between the chapter and the administrator, and with the fact that the patrons of the proposed foundation did not belong to the nobility. The St. Nicholas district, where they intended to found, was one of the most exclusive in the city and would never tolerate a monastery for poor people, built to honour the memory of a mere merchant.

As if this were not bad enough, the late Don Martín's merchant relatives also began to be quite uncooperative. So much so, indeed, that Teresa "broke off negotiations with them entirely" (F. 15,4).

This second difficulty did not trouble Teresa as much as the inability to obtain ecclesiastical permission did. She decided to take the bull by the horns and confront the administrator himself: "I decided to speak with the administrator, so I went to a church near his house and sent a messenger to ask if he would see me. We had been two months trying to get his permission and things were going from bad to worse. When we met, I said it was a shame that women who wanted to live a life of austerity and perfection should be hindered from works which were a great service to Our Lord by those who had no mind for such a life and were living a life of ease. This and plenty more I said to him, for the Lord had made me very determined. His heart was moved, and before I left he gave me the permission" (F. 15,5).

The vision of the administrator of one of the most powerful Sees in Christendom cornered in some obscure sacristy by the forthright logic of an unimportant poor nun says a lot about "God's ways."

Nor is that the end of Teresa's surprising tactics. She was delighted that she had the permission at last, but in reality she still had nothing: neither house nor money to rent one. There were no houses to be had in the city, and Don Martín's executors were not parting with a penny.

Chest used by the Saint to write the "Interior Castle."

It was now that Teresa remembered two people who some time previously had promised help. One was Don Alonso de Avila, a rich merchant; she had not been counting on him for anything because he was very ill at the time. The other was just a "poor student" called Alonso de Andrada. A Franciscan friend of Teresa's had told him to help her if she ever needed any.

As we have indicated, the whole of Toledo had been combed for "a house to let," and not even the most influential of her friends had been able to find anything. Teresa then suggested to her daughters that they entrust the matter to poor Andrada. They laughed; it wouldn't be right for them even to be seen with him, they said. Teresa paid no attention; she was tired of influence that led nowhere. She felt, too, that

there was some mystery about the tattered student's offer of help; so she asked him if he would find a house. "The following morning when I was at Mass in the Jesuit church he came up and told me that he had found a house. He had the keys, he said, and the house was nearby; would we like to go and view it?" (F. 15,7). Imagine the astonishment of the others at this new manifestation of "God's ways," an example of His choosing the weak to confound the strong.

With Don Alonso's money the little house was rented, and the nuns moved in immediately with all their "furniture" — two mattresses, a blanket, some borrowed articles for saying Mass, and a little handbell. In no time, they had the place just as they wanted it. On the 14th they held the official opening in the by now classic Teresian style.

Chalices of St. Teresa's time.

Some time later, Don Martín's famous relatives saw the light, and gave enough money to buy a few houses and build a chapel in honour of St. Joseph. At first the community revelled in the numerous visits from the citizens, but they soon saw that this was disturbing their solitude. Because of this they handed over the church to the chaplains and, thirteen years later, when Beatrice of Jesus, Teresa's niece, was prioress, they moved to their present quarters in what had been Doña Luisa de la Cerda's palace.

So Teresa had yet another dovecote. In Spanish the word 'quinta' means both 'fifth' and 'villa'; Teresa therefore called this, her fifth foundation, her villa. She liked to go there and rest, and enjoyed better health when she did so.

Toledo meant something special to Teresa, as it did to El Greco. They were both there together in 1577 and, according to some scholars, she influenced his brilliant creations with suggestions on subject matter and colouring drawn from her own visions.

How full of paradoxes the story of this foundation has been! Let us dwell briefly on just one of them: the immense paradox that the whole infinite mystery of what we call the Church of Christ should be incarnate in a human and social setup like that of the Toledo church, or any other for that matter. And let us observe Teresa's attitude to the Church.

The Church, as Teresa witnessed it in Toledo, Spain's primatial see, was full of human weakness. The see was, as we have said, without its archbishop at the time. Ten years previously Archbishop Carranza had been arrested by the Inquisition, or rather, by a con-

Seal engraved in steel, used by St. Teresa (Toledo convent).

Toledo Cathedral. View by night. ▷

spiracy of the human frailty of theologians and intellectuals. From prison in Valladolid he was to go on to prison in Rome, never to be reinstated.

It didn't matter that Carranza had been one of the Council Fathers at Trent, that he had been Philip II's adviser on the English question, author of a famous catechism, a friend of spiritual people like Luis de Granada, and a truly spiritual man himself... He fell foul of the great theologians of the day — men like Melchior Cano, Valdés, etc — and that was enough. Ecclesiastically speaking, Toledo was an orphaned church. The cathedral chapter was not on speaking terms with the administrator, since the latter had tried to take over the see. The whole atmosphere was charged with the ecclesiastical class war we alluded to earlier.

How did Teresa react to this situation? She observed and she took action. Teresa observed, read, listened and generally kept herself informed of what was going on in Toledo, and indeed everywhere else as well. The conclusion she came to could not have been more dramatic: "The world is burning; they want to crucify Christ again; they want to tear down the church... No, sisters, this is no time for talking to God of trifling matters" (WP, 1,5).

Teresa took action. She did not waste time on useless lamentations; neither did she do things for the sake of doing something. Having taken note of "the great evils in the Church," she did not raise her voice to denounce them, nor did she condemn bishops and institutions in the style of St. Bridget or St. Catherine of

Siena. She began with her own inner conversion. Then she tried to get others to do the same by dotting the map with her Carmels — each of them the Church in miniature, where chosen souls fought with the arm of prayer "for the defenders of the Church, for the preachers and for the theologians" (WP, 1,3). She would make her nuns the ensigns and standard-bearers in the fight. She would love the Church and fight for it. She would submit each and every grace she received from God to its judgement. Her only ideal would be, as she expressed it on her deathbed, "to be a daughter of the Church."

Proof of this love of Teresa for "the men of her Church" is the litany of ecclesiastical names with which her life is dotted: D. Alvaro de Mendoza, the first father and patron of her work from its beginnings in Avila. Francisco de Ribera, that patriarchal figure of Valencia who asked her to come and personally make a foundation there. D. Fernando de Rojas y Sandoval, the bishop who was hostile when she first went to Seville, but who at a later date would not let her leave until he had first knelt before her and received her blessing. Diego de Leon, the Carmelite bishop who acted as intermediary between herself and the Order. The saintly nuncio, Nicholas Ormaneto, who gave his unreserved support to her work. Even St. Pius V, the Pope to whom Teresa wrote, though both her letter and his answer have been lost.

The list of priests is even longer, many of them the best-known saints and theologians of a period which abounded in both.

And, speaking of knowledge and holiness, let us conclude our little visit to Toledo by pointing out that it was here, on top of that old chest still lovingly preserved by the nuns, that Teresa began the last and most sublime of her works: *The Interior Castle,* or *The Mansions.* Of this monument to man's capacity for experiencing God we shall have occasion to speak later.

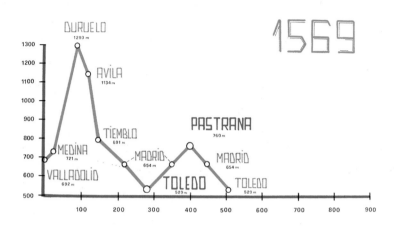

1569

Sketch of the journeys (1569).

[handwritten manuscript text]

"Book of the Foundations" begins to relate the foundation of the Carmelite convents at Pastrana: "Chapter XVII: describes the foundation of the convents at Pastrana of both friars and nuns. The same year MDLXIX."

PASTRANA

St. Teresa's route from Toledo to Pastrana 1569

— May 1569: the Princess of Eboli put pressure on the Saint to found a carmel at Pastrana.
— May 30th: Teresa left Toledo for Pastrana, with a stop in Madrid.
— May 31st: Teresa spent eight days as the guest of the Royal Discalced sisters in Madrid, and met two Italian hermits, Mariano Azzaro and Juan Narduch.
— June 23rd: foundation of the Pastrana Carmel.
— July 10th: the Carmelite friars' monastery was founded at Pastrana. The two Italian hermits took the habit: Mariano de San Benito and Juan de la Miseria.
— July 21st: the Saint returned to Toledo and sent Isabel de Santo Domingo to Pastrana as prioress.

A distressing episode. The Princess of Eboli, Doña Ana de Mendoza, pestered the Saint to let her read the Book of her Life, and succeeded. Later, after a series of conflicts, she was to denounce the book to the Inquisition; the Inquisitors seized it and kept it until after the authoress's death — seven years of uncertainty for Teresa, from 1575 to 1582.

Overall view of Pastrana and, above, convent of the Conceptionists, formerly of the Carmelites. Drawing by Hye Hoys (1866-1867).

PASTRANA (GUADALAJARA)
MONASTERY OF THE CONCEPTION
23.6.1569

This new foundation, which we might well call "Operation Pastrana," is not without its originality.

Against the backdrop of this mountain village, with its olive groves, fig and cherry trees, we shall meet some personages who are not normally part of Teresa's scene. Politics plays a part, bringing with it the interplay of important people, and so does the power of money. It also features the simultaneous founding of houses for both friars and nuns. And, to crown everything, the whole undertaking ends in partial failure.

The story begins in May 1569. Teresa had just put the finishing touches to her Toledo foundation and was enjoying a couple of weeks' peace and quiet. May 29th was Pentecost Sunday and, as Teresa herself tells us:

Façade of the Monastery of the Royal Discalced Nuns (Madrid).

"That morning when we sat down to eat, I was so relieved at having nothing to do and at the prospect of being able to spend some time with the Lord on this Feast that I could hardly eat for happiness. But I mustn't have deserved such consolation, for while we were eating I was told that a servant of the Princess of Eboli, Ruy Gómez de Silva's wife, was outside. I went out to find that the princess had sent for me. She had been trying for quite a while to have one of our monasteries in Pastrana, but I didn't think it would happen so soon. I was troubled, because the monastery I had just founded was so new and still experiencing some opposition that I didn't think it safe to leave it. So I decided not to go, and told him so" (F. 17,2).

The servant was not that easily put off. He had a fine carriage at the door, he said, equipped with everything she would need for the journey. Besides, the princess was already on her way to Pastrana to meet her. Considering the kind of person she was, not to go would be paramount to an insult.

Teresa was in two minds; how could she please everybody? Ruy Gómez was a very valuable friend, and his wife was not a person to be trifled with. She consulted the Lord on the matter and His word was to go; that there was much more than just a foundation involved here. Her confessor confirmed this view, and her mind was made up.

"I left Toledo on Whit Monday. Our journey took us through Madrid, where my companions and I stayed

with some Franciscan nuns. The lady who founded that convent was also living with them; she was Doña Leonor de Mascareñas, who had at one time been the King's governess'' (F. 17,5).

It is worth noting here that up until then Teresa's reforming enterprise had never had political overtones. Reforming was quite fashionable at the time, and there were two clear centres of reformist activity: Rome and Madrid. Rome's vision was ecclesiastical; that of Madrid had a distinctly political slant. Teresa's work was done through the Carmelite Prior General in Rome and belonged to the first category. The nearest her work had ever come to involvement with the Court was her tiff with the Council of Avila about the wells near St. Joseph's.

Soon, however, thanks to the Pastrana house, she was to become involved in that little world of powerful people. It is they who now seem to take the initiative in founding; who place the means at her disposal: who get their own interests mixed up in it; who change Teresa's habitual procedure by substituting plush carriages for muleback or caravan, page boys for muleteers, dealings with the mighty for the simple but effective Andradas of this world. In this undertaking Teresa would not have to dirty her hands along with plasterers and masons. All this, let us add, unwillingly and in obedience to the Voice within.

That said, let us return to her in the convent of the Royal Reformed sisters she was staying with. Teresa conversed with Doña Leonor and was introduced by her to two strange hermits, of whom more later. Among those who came to visit her was King Philip II's own sister, Doña Juana de Austria, widow of Don Juan of Portugal. Teresa would appear to have made a good impression on the princess, for she was afterwards very helpful when Teresa had to deal with the King.

The kind of environment in which Teresa moved dur-

Overall view of Pastrana and the convent of the Carmelite friars.

The nuns' convent.

Convent and hermitage of St. Peter.

ing her stay in Madrid is best summed up in the following anecdote about a group of high-ranking ladies who, at the Princess of Eboli's invitation, came to see the famous nun from Toledo. To quote a contemporary chronicler: "Many of the leading ladies of Madrid high society came to see her; some out of devotion, others out of curiosity. Some wanted to witness a miracle, others wanted to know the future. Oh, the natural weakness of women! But Teresa's humility was more than equal to such a situation. She spoke simply and plainly to them, and, after the initial polite exchanges were over, she steered the conversation to such neutral subjects as the beauty of the streets of Madrid, etc."

Teresa spent a week in Madrid. No doubt she also conversed with the nuns and influenced them to some degree with her approach and outlook. She certainly made a very favourable impression, as the following passage written by the Abbess, Juana de la Cruz, testifies: "Praise God who has permitted us to see a saint whom we can imitate. She eats, sleeps and speaks like the rest of us, and is completely natural and unassuming."

Towards June, just before Corpus Christi, the founding party set off at last for Pastrana: two nuns, the chaplain, Fr. Pedro Muriel, and Beatriz de Cisneros — a servant of Doña Leonor's who was thinking of taking the habit. In the princess's fast and comfortable coach the journey was pleasant and short: two days. Through Alcalá, Villalbilla, Pezuela and along the Tagus valley to Pastrana. This little town was just then at the height of its glory. Centred on the proud palace of its princely family, it had a population of 827 souls in and around it.

Before going on with the story, let us meet this princely couple, for to understand the story one must be acquainted with these two personages.

Doña Ana de Mendoza y de la Cerda, the princess, was twenty-nine years old at the time. Some described her as "out of her mind"; others as "a furious and formidable woman." What is certain is that as the only daughter of a very powerful family she was accustomed from childhood to giving free rein to her every whim. Depending on what suited her, she could be aggressive, insolent, astute, flattering, generous or a prude. Perhaps she did have some honesty and piety deep down; so deep down that they were covered over by her other qualities.

Ruy Gómez, her husband, on the other hand, was the soul of discretion, and always struggling to tone down his strident wife. Portuguese by birth, he had, nevertheless, found great favour with the King. Maybe that is why a contemporary said of him that "After the glory of his God, his only other object in life is the happiness of his King."

Now that we have introduced our hosts, let us continue. Teresa and her companions were given a truly princely and unforgettable welcome. Still, even now she was beginning to feel there was something in the whole atmosphere of the place which would eventually sour their stay here: certain ridiculous demands of the princess, who seemed to regard the nuns as a new toy to play with.

The princess tried to determine to what degree they should be poor, the size of their cells, their daily routine, which novices were suitable, and a whole lot of other things which Teresa regarded as her own business. Title, money, favours done, or promised, gave the princess no right to change the nuns' lifestyle in the slightest.

Heated discussions took place in the ornate drawing-room of the palace; the princess threatening, Teresa letting it be known she would just go back to Madrid without making any foundation; the prince, once more, tempering his wife's demands.

Teresa was full of bitter presentiments, but she carried on chiefly because she wanted to see a second house of her discalced friars there.

After many difficulties the monastery was inaugurated on 23 June 1569. With great tact and prudence, and on Teresa's orders making a note of every last thing donated by the princess, the sisters survived the next four years. And then Ruy Gómez died. That completely unhinged the princess and she decided to join the Carmelites! Nor was there any arguing with this decision. She took the habit, but her character remained the same. Though junior to the rest, she tried to have her way in everything, and was consequently expelled. She returned to her palace determined to avenge herself. She had tricked Teresa into letting her have a copy of her *Life,* and she now made little of it privately and in public. Not only that, she denounced the book to the Inquisition, took back everything she had given the nuns, broke the endowment contract, and subjected them to whatever humiliation she could think of.

To put an end to so sorry a state of affairs, Teresa told her nuns to leave Pastrana a year later. She took them to Segovia instead.

Now, as we've mentioned, the fact that Teresa was trying to make a male foundation as well as a female one was always a complicating factor in the Pastrana undertaking. She had permission from the Prior General for two such foundations. One was already established in Duruelo; she had planned the other for Pastrana.

This is where the two characters she was introduced to in Madrid by Doña Leonor come in. Both were Italians; one was called Mariano Azzaro, the other Giovanni Narduch. According to Teresa, the former was "a doctor and very ingenious"; the latter, more imaginative and artistic. Both were half pilgrims, half hermits. Always in search of a place of austere solitude, with the help of Doña Leonor and Ruy Gómez they eventually ended up in Pastrana, where the latter gave them a hermitage to fulfil their cherished dreams.

Descent to the hermits' grottos.

Palace of the Prince and Princess of Eboli.

For Teresa, to meet two hermits who had a hermitage in Pastrana was an obvious act of Providence. Here is how she described her interview with Mariano:
"When he described his way of life to me, I showed him a copy of our Primitive Rule, and told him he would have little trouble in observing all of it; it was the same as his way of life, especially where manual work was concerned... When I explained how much he could serve the Lord in our habit, he said he would think about it that night... His Majesty loved him, and so moved him that on the following day he called me and told me his mind was made up. The speed with which he changed his mind surprised him, especially since it was a woman who changed it for him" (F. 17,9).

When Mariano changed his mind, so did Juan. Before leaving Pastrana, therefore, Teresa obtained the Provincial's permission to convert the hermitage into a friary; the above two and a Fr. Baltasar de Jesús constituting the community. That happened on 13 July of the same year. Mariano took San Benito as his religious surname; Giovanni Narduch became Juan de la Miseria, the name with which he was later to sign his famous portrait of Mother Teresa.

Stated so briefly, all this sounds a lot simpler and more straightforward than it was in reality. This house was to cause Teresa more than its share of heartaches. Removed from their favourite state of being solitary hermits, encouraged by fashionable extremes then in vogue — including the extravagances of a certain Catalina de Cardona, of whom more in a moment — and lacking in the wisdom and prudence that accompanied the kind of sanctity that John of the Cross had established at Duruelo, they soon slipped into a pitiless form of penance which had a strong influence on the newly-founded Discalced Carmelite friars. Nevertheless, there were Carmelite Friars in Pastrana until the expulsion of the religious in 1835. Today, their house (much altered) is occupied by Franciscans.

The Saint gives fray A. Mariano the rules of the Reform. ▷

negia.

V.P.E.AMBROSIO M.RIANO ITALIANO DY LVS RELINGEDOC.REN AMB DO
RECH O ELOCVENT. ID GR. VIRTVDS ASISTIO A.S. CON. D REN
TOR A JOLE A. ORD NN RAS. M.TERESA PA. A FVNDAR EL COMB. D PAST.
LE EN GRANDCE POR.LO MVCHO Q. RA A JO EN EL DSCA CE Z FV
PRIME R E RECTOR DLA PROBINCIA D POR. TVGA.M. EN M. CONA
IS ENCIA DLOS M R.S.S. COM E IS. DAMIANEL AÑO D 1594

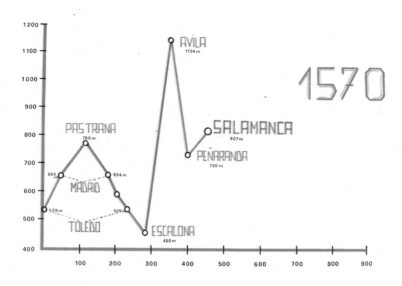

1570

Sketch of the journey to Salamanca.

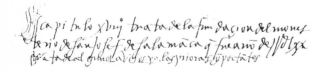

"Book of the Foundations," begins to relate the foundation of the Carmelite convent in Salamanca: "Chapter XVIII: describes the foundation of the convent of St. Joseph in Salamanca, in the year MDLXX. Deals with important advice for the prioresses..."

SALAMANCA

St. Teresa's route
from Toledo to Salamanca
1570

— May. 1570: the community in Toledo moved, to the Ramírez house.
— July 10th: the Saint returned to Pastrana and attended the taking of vows by Mariano de San Benito and Fray Juan de la Miseria.
— mid-August: Teresa set out from Toledo to Avila and Salamanca.
— October 31st: she arrived in Salamanca.
— November 1st: the carmel in Salamanca was founded. The night at the "students' house."
— the same day: the Carmelites founded their college at Alcalá de Henares.

The pace of foundations had escalated. Salamanca and Alcalá were the most important university cities of the time — seats of learning, and a crossroads for Spanish youth. For her part, Mother Teresa was "in favour of learning"; in her language, "learning" meant Biblical and humanistic culture. She was a great admirer of scholars: "I have never been deceived by a learned man," she wrote. At the same time as founding a carmel in Salamanca, she succeeded in establishing a College for her young friars in Alcalá; soon she sent Fray John of the Cross as its rector. She also struggled incessantly to set up another house of study in Salamanca; she was to succeed towards the end of her life (1581). Both colleges were to attain fame, for their celebrated "Salamanca Courses" (in theology) and "Alcalá Course" (in philosophy).

View of the old Carmelite convent in Salamanca, drawing by Hye Hoys.

SALAMANCA
ST. JOSEPH'S MONASTERY
1.11.1570.

In his popular *Life of St. Teresa,* the late Fr. Crisógono de Jesús, one of the finest modern writers of spiritual literature in Spanish, summed up the story of one of Teresa's costliest foundations in this fine passage:

''Four months have passed, and it is All Souls' Night 1570 in Salamanca. The city is subdued as a hundred bells ring out from churches and monasteries, sounding like one long groan from souls floating restlessly above their belfries and towers.

In an empty mansion to the north of the city two nuns are busy barring ill-fitting doors and windows. They are Mother Teresa and Sister María del Sacramento, just arrived from Avila after a cold, wet journey. They have come to make a foundation. A few moments earlier the old mansion was shaking in the uproar caused by students who were refusing to hand over to the nuns. Now the great old building, with its large rooms, wide passages, and endless attics was silent once more. The funeral toll of the city bells and the howling wind came through the crevices in the windows, sighing and moaning.

Teresa's companion is afraid: afraid of the students, some of whom could still be hiding in any nook or cranny; afraid of the dead, groaning among the towers. Teresa laughs at her frightened sister, who keeps looking over her shoulder as if she expected the shadows to creep up on her, or ghosts to come in without opening the door.

At last, the long, hard day took its toll and they settled themselves down on some straw to sleep, covered with a few old borrowed blankets. Sister María was still restless. She thought of the dead and looked round every time a board creaked.

"What are you looking at?", asked Teresa. "Can't you see that nobody can come in?"

"Mother," she replied, "I was thinking what would you do here alone if I were to die now."

"Sister, if that happens I'll think of something. Right now, just let me get some sleep."

Minutes later, the two nuns were sound asleep on their bed of straw, snug in their borrowed blankets.

At dawn, all fears and shadows gone, they are up and assembling a modest wooden altar. They tidy up passages, rooms, and stairs, left in a mess by the students. The first Mass is celebrated, and the foundation is established. Saint Teresa is happy in her rambling, old mansion and pokes fun at Sister María about her fears of the night before."

The Salamanca undertaking, however, was not as funny as that; nor did it take place so quickly.

From Pastrana Teresa had gone to Toledo, a place she always found stimulating and where, indeed, she either began or wrote her greatest works. Then on to Avila, because the bishop was becoming a little alarmed at the length of her absence from a community of which she was prioress.

"While I was attending to this, the Jesuit Rector at Salamanca wrote to me, giving me reasons why it would be good to have one of our monasteries in that city" (F. 18,1).

Trusting in her unfailing God rather than in the reasons given her; trusting, too, in her hard-working and poverty-loving nuns who needed little to live on, and in the good offices of loyal friends like the merchant Nicolás Gutiérrez (father of many nuns, including some Carmelites), she decided to embark on yet another foundation.

The more experienced she became in this business of foundations, the more cautious Teresa became. This time she asked the bishop of Salamanca's permission before leaving Avila. The Jesuit Rector, who had achieved a certain amount of fame as a chronicler of the Council of Trent, obtained this for her immediately. Another precaution she took was not to bring her nuns with her, thus avoiding the risk of finding herself without a house for them, as happened at Medina. This time she went with just one companion, to make sure that the house rented by Fr. Julián of Avila was in order.

She set out for Salamanca, accompanied by two Carmelite Fathers of the Observance. Seventeen leagues and several stops later they reached their destination. "We arrived on the vigil of All Saints, having travelled much of the way by night and in bitter cold... I was not at all well" (F. 18,3).

She must have been pretty ill, because it was only when writing of this foundation that she alluded to the physical hardships of her founding expeditions: "When describing these foundations I don't say anything of the hardships endured along the way: the cold, the heat and the snow. At times it snowed all day, sometimes we got lost, other times I was so ill

University of Salamanca, with the Cathedral in the
background.

and feverish. Praise God, my health is usually poor,
but I've always been conscious that God was giving
me strength'' (F. 18,4).

It was here in Salamanca, by order of Fr. Ripalda, that
Teresa began writing *The Book of the Foundations,* a
book she would go on writing to within a few days of
her death. Here, with the simplicity of genius, she
tells the story of her reforming work, the bad
moments as well as the good, from the first to the last
foundation. Its pages are a hymn of praise to God,
praise expressed through events in which He took
part. They must be read in the same spirit of praise in
which they were written. A copy in Teresa's own
hand is in the Escorial Library.

Monument to fray Luis de León in front of the University.

Courtyard of "St. Teresa's House" (Salamanca).

"Ecce Homo," painting bought by St. Teresa for the Salamanca foundation.

Salamanca's claim to fame rests on its University. Its 7,000 students provided the country with an unending flow of cardinals, bishops, Council Fathers, viceroys, inquisitors, royal counsellors, and all the other brains of the social and political élite that ruled half the world and enhanced the name of the city.

That is the good side. Its halls were also the sounding board for a thousand and one problems from all over the Kingdom, from Rome and the Americas. The tensions of the age left their mark on the cloisters, and the academic climate was highly polemical.

To give just one example, in 1561 Fray Luis de León translated the *Song of Songs* from the original Hebrew. In 1570 he was expounding his theories on the Latin translation (known as the Vulgate) in opposition to León de Castro, an enemy of the Hebrew specialists. The hall he lectured in still stands. In 1571 Bartolomé de Medina — a close friend of St. Teresa's — drew up a list of 17 statements attributed to Fray Luis, resulting in the latter's imprisonment by the Inquisition from March 1572 to 1576. When he regained his freedom, Fray Luis returned to the lecture hall with the celebrated phrase: "As we were saying yesterday...."

A lively student world, therefore. And Teresa arrived in the middle of it just about the time students returned for the new academic year. It was not the easiest time to find a house to rent. She solved this problem, as we've seen, and with the little money she had with her she bought two important items of furniture for the new foundation: a painting of the Ecce Homo and a painting of Our Lady receiving Christ from the Cross.

They were not long in their old mansion before it became obvious that it had certain drawbacks. The building itself was not very sound, but its situation was an even greater handicap — its proximity to a river and the city reservoir made life intolerable. Soon, the health of the community was affected, and the house was declared to be unfit to house the Blessed Sacrament. This was the last straw; it was time to consider moving.

We have to pause here, however, and allow Teresa to attend to other business before the move can be attended to. Business took her to Alba; some very unpleasant difficulties required her presence in the Medina and Avila houses for a time; and she was even called upon to make peace in her old monastery of the Incarnation. Then she returned.

After a rather eventful journey — once the mule that carried the money got lost, and another time the whole group — Teresa reached Salamanca on 13 July 1571. The party first visited the house which they intended buying. It lay between Plaza de San Benito and Calle de los Doctrinos, the latter now named after the Jesuits. It was owned by a man called Pedro de la Vanda, but legal formalities were holding up proceedings. Teresa was in a hurry, since the new lessees of the mansion were putting pressure on the nuns to leave. Fortunately, the owner allowed Teresa to proceed with the rather substantial alterations which were needed. Getting the house ready was going to take a long time.

The little community spent all they had (i.e. all their dowries) turning this building into a monastery, complete with cloister, cells, refectory and chapel. And Teresa still found the money to buy an ornate "reredos depicting Our Lady, with St. Joseph on one side and St. Bartholomew on the other, and including both God the Father and St. Mary Magdalen as well." Quite a treasure at the time, apparently.

With this heavenly court installed, all was ready for the inauguration. This time quite a solemn one. "There was a large congregation present and we had music; the Blessed Sacrament was installed with great solemnity" (F. 19,10). The preacher for the occasion was the best the city could boast of, their Chrysostom, Diego de Estella.

Teresa's troubles were, nevertheless, far from over. "The very next day — to temper our joy at having the Blessed Sacrament — the owner of the house came. He was so angry I didn't know what to do with him; and it must have been the devil who made sure he couldn't see reason, for we had fulfilled all the conditions in the contract. I decided to leave him the house; but he didn't want that either" (F. 19,10).

What Pedro de la Vanda, or rather his wife who put him up to it, really wanted was money "to settle two daughters." The contract had not required payment of this money until the King's solution to the legal technicalities was obtained.

Writing about this three years after the event, St. Teresa remarked that the purchase had not yet been finalised. In fact it took forty-four years, during which they were twice evicted, before the nuns were finally established in that house.

No wonder Teresa wrote: "In no monastery of this first Rule have the nuns suffered anything like the trials they had in this one" (F.19,12).

Happily it was in Salamanca too that the Lord granted her very clear proof of His help and many mystical graces.

Chief instrument of His help was Fr. Gutiérrez, S.J. It was he who invited her to Salamanca. He and his fellow Jesuits welcomed her and used all their influence in her favour. Above all, she was able to talk openly to him about everything, and sometimes spent whole evenings with him just talking about God. Soon, however, that Father fell victim to the French Huguenots and was sorely missed by Teresa: "God help me, I wish I wasn't so fond of God's servants; then I wouldn't miss them so much."

As for mystical graces, they were so frequent about this time that it was difficult to hide their external effects. According to the testimony of Isabel de Jesús: "When she heard me sing a little couplet expressing a longing for God, she was so enraptured that after a time she had to be carried back to her cell in a state of apparent unconsciousness." The couplet in question was:

> Would that my eyes could see You,
> Kind Sweet Jesus,
> Would that my eyes could see You,
> And I then died.

That then is the story of yet another seedbed; the story of how the Teresian seed took root in the hostile soil of this Mecca of Learning, the great Salamanca. One of the characteristic features of Teresian spirituality is, in fact, an esteem for learning. It is worth dwelling on this for a moment, since we happen to be talking of her presence in a seat of learning. Many influences went into the formation of Teresa's teachings. The most important and the most obvious is that of God Himself. But the oral teachings of many learned men of the time certainly had a strong influence on her too.

She was in touch with the best theologians and consulted the best qualified confessors, many of whom are mentioned in the course of these pages. She also knew people as famous for their sanctity as Juan de Avila and Fray Luis de León, and was on intimate terms with souls as wholly heavenly as that of John of the Cross. All these encounters met a ready response in her fertile mind and heart. All left their mark, even if not equally, and for this she was eternally grateful to all of them.

Since she assumed that she was only an ignorant woman, she looked to them all for teaching, discernment, security and support. And that not just for herself, but for her daughters and anyone else who wanted to follow her counsels. These are the kind of things she said about learned men:

"I have never been deceived by a learned man."

Façade of the church of St. Andrew (former convent of Carmelite friars in Salamanca).

"I have always been, and will continue to be, of the opinion that a Christian should try, if at all possible, to converse with a learned man; and the more learned the better."

"I never did anything without first consulting learned men."

Fr. Domingo Báñez, one of her favourite confessors, once remarked: "She preferred learned men to those who were merely pious."

Fierce controversy raged in her day between theologians and "spirituals." She was undoubtedly one of the latter, among whom she had many close friends. But she sided with the theologians. They, she thought, have the Bible, theology and philosophy — all she understood by "learning" — and these things were "light." Still, she would not like the theologian to speak from hearsay; she wanted him grounded in experience. Theoreticians were not not her cup of tea.

Teresa took the best of both extremes; she teaches on the basis of both. She is brimming with experience, yet hungry for the light which books and theologians can throw on it. That is how she came to be a Doctor of the Church.

In the last years of her life, she was thrilled to see the Discalced Carmelite friars also founding in Salamanca, and sending their students to the university. In her last letter to Fr. Gracián she told him that students should not be overburdened with either tasks or penances that would interfere with their studies.

St. Teresa's confessional in St. Stephen's, Salamanca.

Magnificent Renaissance façade of St. Stephen's church (Dominicans).

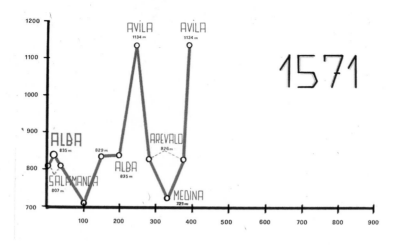

1571

Sketch of the Saint's journeys in 1571: from Salamanca to Alba and Avila.

The "Book of the Foundations" begins to relate the foundation of the Carmelite convent of Alba "Chapter XX: describes the foundation of the convent of Our Lady of the Annunciation in Alba de Tormes. In the year MDLXXI."

ALBA

St. Teresa's route
Salamanca — Alba — Avila
1571

— October 26th 1569: Pope Pius V named the Dominican Pedro Fernández as Visitator of the Carmelites in Castile.
— December 3rd 1570: deeds for the foundation of the convent at Alba.
— January 25th 1571: the Alba carmel was founded, in the presence of Fray John of the Cross.
— early February: Teresa returned to Salamanca.
— April 6th: Rubeo formalised further permits for Mother Teresa to continue founding.
— April 15th (Easter): at recreation, the novice Sister Isabel sang the couplets "Would that my eyes could see You," and the Saint went into rapture.
— April: journey to Medina; and from there to Avila.
— July 10th: St Teresa accepted the post of prioress of the Incarnation convent at Avila, appointed by the Visitator.
— August-September: at the Medina carmel once again.
— early October: Mother Teresa returned from Medina to Avila. On October 6th she took up her appointment as prioress at the Incarnation — for 3 years.
— March 25th 1572: Jerónimo Gracián, who was later to be the Teresian Reform's provincial, took his vows at Pastrana.

Historical background. Events: *a lull in the religious wars in France (Treaty of Saint Germain: 1570). — Religious persecution in England: excommunication of Queen Elizabeth (1570). — Battle of Lepanto (1571). — The "St. Bartholomew's Night Massacre" (France, 23-24/8/1572). Personalities: St Pius V and St Francis Borgia died in Rome (1572). — The trial of Fray Luis de León began in Salamanca (1572).*

Exterior of the convent, Alba: drawing by Hye Hoys (1866-1867).

ALBA DE TORMES (SALAMANCA)
MONASTERY OF THE ANNUNCIATION
25.1.1571

Like Salamanca, Alba is on the right bank of the river Tormes. But Alba, thanks to its upstream position, married the Tormes and took its surname, so to speak.

Only a small plateau, crossed by an ancient Roman paved highway, separates them. Two little hamlets punctuate the sixteen mile journey, and then the slow descent begins through gently undulating countryside to the Tormes, dominating the fertile plain below, a plain that stretches away to the Sierra de Gredos on the horizon.

Just before the final descent the view is magnificent. To the right, the Hieronymite monastery of St. Leonard with its Gothic church and splendid colonnade. Beyond, the belfries and steeples of parish and convent churches rise above the houses. And, on a

"St. Teresa's spring," on
the way to Alba...

Partial view part of Alba
de Tormes, with the river
in the foreground.

The house of Saint Teresa.

St. Teresa's Basilica, Alba. Unfinished.

promontory, the proud castle of the Dukes of Alba, with its six gilded towers, is beautifully framed against the bright blue sky of Castile. The medieval bridge, with its twenty-six arches spanning the Tormes, completes the picture.

In Teresa's day the Duke of Alba was one of the most important men in the realm. So great was his influence with Philip II that even men like the aforementioned Prince of Eboli could reach the King only through him.

However, he had nothing to do with Teresa's coming to Alba. Neither did she come because she liked the idea of founding there. "I was not very enthusiastic about it, because being a small town the community would need an endowment, and I preferred not to have any" (F. 20,1).

The request came from a couple in Salamanca — D. Francisco Velázquez, the University Bursar, and his wife Doña Teresa de Layz, who was a native of Alba. Her sister and brother-in-law had a hand in it too; they were friends of the above couple and lived nearby.

Teresa goes into great detail about how this couple came to want a monastery of Discalced Carmelite nuns. So let us hear the story.

Teresa Layz was born into a Castilian family, but she was not exactly welcomed. "Her parents had already had four children, all girls. When they saw that the fifth, Teresa Layz, was yet another daughter they were very upset" (F. 20,2).

As a result of this disappointment and human weakness, the child received very little attention in the first days of her life. "Things got so bad that, as if they didn't care whether the child lived or not, they left her alone all day when she was only three days old. One good thing they had done: they had had her baptized by a priest when she was born. That evening a woman who was concerned, and knew what was going on, ran to see if she was dead. Others who had

Castle of the Duke of Alba.

Façade of the church, Carmelite convent of Alba.

come to visit the mother followed her and were witnesses to what I am now about to relate.

The woman took the crying baby in her arms and said: 'Now, now, little one, are you not a Christian?', referring to the cruelty with which she had been treated. The baby raised her head and said: 'Yes, I am.' She didn't speak again until the normal age at which children start talking. Those who heard her were astonished, and from then on her mother began to love and cherish her. She often said afterwards that she wanted to live long enough to see what God had in store for this child.''

The first thing God did was to provide her with a husband who, as well as being virtuous and rich, doted on his wife. ''He sought her pleasure in everything. And well he might, for the Lord gave her everything a husband could ask for in a wife'' (F. 20,5). The husband was D. Francisco Velázquez.

The only thing which God had apparently omitted to give this exemplary couple was children, in spite of how much they wanted them and prayed for them. Doña Teresa prayed specially to St. Andrew with this intention.

Time passed, until one day ''the lady, still as anxious as ever to have a family, seemed to see herself in a house which had a well in the courtyard beneath the gallery. She also saw a green meadow with white flowers all through it, beautiful beyond description. St. Andrew appeared beside the well, as a venerable and handsome old man... ''The children you will have are different to those you desire,'' he said... She understood clearly... that it was God's will that she should found a monastery'' (F. 20,7).

Providence, all unknown to us, weaves the fabric of our lives. And into this fabric He now wove another thread: the Duchess of Alba decided that she would like the University Bursar to look after the financial management of her estates. One did not refuse the

The Carmelites' refectory.

Interior of the convent, Alba.

St. Teresa's cell.

Duchess, and so it was that D. Francisco came to move from Salamanca to Alba, for less interesting work and a poorer house.

But, what was Doña Teresa's surprise when on taking possession of the house she found it was the house she had seen in her vision, complete with courtyard and well! This so moved her that "she decided to turn it into a monastery."

All that remained now was to choose her "adopted family" from among the great variety of Orders that existed. Someone, apparently inspired by the devil, said that nuns should be ruled out as "most of them were discontent people." A Franciscan friar, however, suggested that Mother Teresa's nuns seemed to fit Doña Teresa's description of what she was looking for. "Between ourselves and the Hieronymites," he said, "this place has enough friars." The fact that Doña Teresa was looking for a small, austere, strictly enclosed community certainly pointed in the direction of the Carmelites. The fact that their famous foundress was only down the road in Salamanca, and that her sister was a friend of the founding couple, clinched the issue.

"At last agreement was reached and an adequate endowment arranged. What impressed me most was that they left their own house to us and moved to a humbler one themselves. The Blessed Sacrament was reserved and the foundation made on the Feast of St. Paul's Conversion 1571" (F.20,14). Teresa had now reached the half-way stage of her foundations; she was fifty-six.

At the beginning of ch. 20, devoted to the Alba foundation, Teresa complained of one thing: the attitude of people who, ignorant of God's purpose, behave like Doña Teresa's parents in their resentment at having daughters rather than sons. They do so because they fail to realise the great benefits that having daughters can bring or the great harm that having sons can bring; they are unwilling to leave everything

The Monastery viewed form the garden.

Relics. Container for holy water which St. Teresa used to take with her.

to Him who understands everything. "How many fathers will go to Hell for having had sons, and how many mothers will go to Heaven on account of the daughters they had!" (F.20,3).

This little outburst of Teresa's provides us with an opportunity to say something about her feminism.

Today, people are very sensitive about neglected sectors of society and there is consequently a strong protest on behalf of the rights of such people. Teresa was very conscious of the fact that the women of her time belonged to this category; that they were discriminated against because of their sex. Moreover, there was no way they could fight this. So, in ch. 3 of the *Way of Perfection,* Teresa launched a spirited defence of women, appealing even to Christ's judgement. The censor erased this from the first edition, but now it is restored and we can read the truly prophetic passage for ourselves:

"When you walked on this earth, Lord, you did not despise women; rather, you always helped them and showed great compassion towards them. And you found as much love and more faith in them than you did in men. Among them was your Most Blessed Mother, and through her merits we merit what, because of our offences, we do not deserve. Is it not enough, Lord, that the world has intimidated us... so that we may not do anything worthwhile for you in public or dare to speak some truths that we lament over in secret, without your also failing to hear so just a petition? I do not believe, Lord, that this could be true of your goodness and justice, for you are a just judge and not like those of the world. Since the world's judges are sons of Adam and all of them men, there is no virtue in women that they do not hold suspect" (WP.3,9).

She was supported in her opinion that women were as valuable in God's eyes as men were by men of such proven sanctity as St. Peter of Alcántara. In fact, speaking to Teresa, he went even further than she: "God grants His favours to many more women than men," he said. He added that they made far greater progress in the way of prayer and he gave many reasons in favour of women (V.40,8).

Day after day she saw for herself how God showered His favours on her dovecotes just as soon as they filled up. How, then, was one to explain why men kept women in the wings of the socio-religious stage when God Himself seemed determined to give them leading roles?

Teresa was fully aware of her own unimportance. She even had a bit of a complex about it, always saying she was frail and ignorant. But she loved learning, as we've seen, and highly esteemed learned men. She would stand no second-class citizenship in the world of knowledge; she and her daughters would be trained, educated in what concerned their way of life. She learned from theologians and confessors, and, in turn, taught her sisters, orally and through the written word. As time went on, she attached increasing importance to this.

She spelled out clearly the role her sisters were to play in society and in the Church. She thought big: the universal Church was to be the object of their prayers, thoughts and mortifications.

If we look at the dominant theme of today's feminism — the feeling that women have "come of age" and are on an equal footing with their traditional tutors, men; that they are equals in will and courage — we find it abundantly foreshadowed in Teresa's thinking. Teresa's fearlessness is proverbial, legendary even. Normally she shunned self-praise, but where courage was concerned she admitted: "They say I have no little courage, and it has been seen that God has given me more than is usual in a woman" (L.8,7).

She lived in vigorous times, times charged with the exploits of conquistadores who conquered new worlds for their King. But it was always men who did these things. And the word "man" came to conjure up a picture of courage, effort, daring, and capacity for making sacrifices. Teresa fought against the monopolising of these "manly" qualities by men; they were human qualities and just as much within the capabilities of women as of men. "The Lord will make them so manly that they will astonish men," she said of her nuns (WP.7,8).

Teresa's life is full of examples of her determination. From the time when, as a child, she convinced her brother to go off with her to be beheaded by the Moors for Christ to the time when, as an adult, she committed her life fully to Christ, Teresa's life is full of examples of her characteristic determination. Whenever she was faced with a difficulty, her attitude was always the same: "It is very important to be quite determined not to stop till you reach the end of the road, no matter what happens, what it costs, or what anybody says... even if you die in the attempt... or if the world itself should come to an end" (WP.21,1).

All her courage and daring had a solid foundation, however; much more solid than that of many modern feminists who, without it, may find it difficult to last the pace. That foundation was the love of her God. All that mattered to Teresa was to know that whatever she undertook was God's will. To find this out she prayed and sought advice; but once she knew, "forward" was her only gear.

When people sympathised with her in her difficulties; when people saw her ill-health and urged her to rest and leave aside this troublesome business of founding monasteries, she would smile and say "That wouldn't be loving God, would it?"

That, then, is Teresa's style of feminism. A love for being a woman; something born of her admiration for her mother Doña Beatriz, and developed by her devotion to Mary, blessed among women.

Church and altarpiece of the convent, Alba. In the centre, behind the altar, the tomb of the Saint.

Some of the women who helped her deserve to be called co-foundresses of her monasteries: Doña Guiomar de Ulloa in Avila; Doña Luisa de la Cerda in Malagón; Doña María de Mendoza in Valladolid; Doña Teresa de Layz here in Alba; or Doña Catalina de Tolosa in Burgos. There were others who went a step further and took the habit themselves: Doña Ana Jimena in Segovia and Doña Catalina de Sandoval in Beas.

She had a train of admirers: Queen Juana of Portugal; nobility such as Doña Leonor de Mascareñas; famous penitents like la Cardona; simple housewives like Juana Dantisco, Fr. Gracián's mother; and humble village folk too numerous to mention.

The names of certain children have also become associated with Teresa's memory: there was her niece, Teresita, Lorenzo's daughter and later a nun under Teresa's guidance in the Seville Carmel; Fr. Gracián's sister Isabel in the Toledo Carmel; and Antonio Gaytán's daughter, who was admitted to this Alba monastery at the tender age of seven. Teresa lavished affection on all of these, seeing in them future strong women who would, no doubt, put the fear of God into the strong men of Castile.

A far more difficult task is to single out the more prominent of her early Carmelite sisters. Yet there are a few names that must be mentioned: María de San José, Salazar, the prioress of Seville is one: she has left us an accurate portrait of the Saint in her writings, and perhaps reproduced it even more accurately in her own life. Anne of Jesus, Lobera, was so outstanding that St. John of the Cross dedicated his *Spiritual Canticle* to her, as did Fray Luis de León his edition of *St. Teresa's Works.* María Bautista, that intelligent niece who suggested the idea of the reform to her. Anne of St. Bartholomew, her nurse and scribe, who afterwards took the Order to France and

Her greatest reward in this area was that marvellous and select group of women which gathered round her "to do what little they could" to solve the evils that beset the Church.

Statue of St. Teresa. Monument to the Saint in Alba.

View of Alba.

Façade of the church of the Carmelite friars (Alba).

Flanders (together with Anne of Jesus) and is today among those honoured by the Church as Blessed. María de Jesús, who Teresa used jokingly to call her "little scholar," and has also been beatified. These and many more constitute her crown and glory both as a saint and as a woman.

But, as Teresa herself would say, we digress. A worthwhile digression, however. Nor have we finished with Alba: how Teresa came to die here; the description of her famous relics, and a few other matters deserve separate treatment. They will constitute the last chapter of this story.

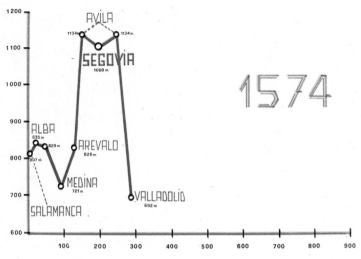

Sketch of the journey to Segovia, and from Segovia to Valladolid.

Foundation of the Carmelite convent in Segovia in the "Book of the Foundations": "Chapter XXI: tells of the foundation of the convent of the glorious St. Joseph in Segovia. It was founded on the feast of St. Joseph in the year MDLXXIIII."

SEGOVIA

St. Teresa's route as Prioress of the Incarnation at Avila 1571-1574

— *spring 1572: Teresa took Fray John of the Cross as confessor to the Incarnation convent in Avila.*
— *February 1573: journey to Alba and Salamanca.*
— *August 25th: Mother Teresa began the* Book of the Foundations *in Salamanca.*
— *September 28th: the Salamanca community moved to Pedro de la Vanda's houses.*
— *March 1574: St. Teresa left Alba for Segovia, accompanied by St. John of the Cross; they arrived on March 18th.*
— *March 19th: foundation of the Segovia carmel.*
— *April 6th-7th: the nuns from Pastrana arrived at Segovia, having left the foundation in the hands of the Princess of Eboli.*
— *September 30th: the Saint set out from Segovia for Avila.*
— *October 6th: the end of her term as prioress of the Incarnation at Avila.*
— *late December: Teresa travelled to Valladolid because of Casilda de Padilla and her family's dispute.*

A woman's leadership. — *Suddenly, Mother Teresa found herself in charge of a heterogeneous group, and responsible for a vast spiritual movement. Without claiming the juridical or formal command for herself, she was in fact mother, teacher, leader, and the living incarnation of the group's ideals. She knew how to surround herself with people of worth, and raised them to positions of responsibility. She travelled so as to be present in the most difficult advances. By letter she kept up an open dialogue with all parties, based on friendship, teaching and leadership.*

*Exterior of the convent, Segovia: drawing by Hye Hoys
(1866-1867).*

SEGOVIA
MONASTERY OF ST JOSEPH OF
CARMEL
19.3.1574

Just as formerly Castile had expanded at the pace of
El Cid's horse, so now Carmel was expanding in the
wake of Teresa's covered wagon.

Nevertheless, there were those who looked upon its
progress as if it were a kind of oil slick spreading un-
stoppable across the broad plains of Castile. For
such, Teresa's reform was like a wound which would
soon infect the whole organism if someone did not
quickly put a stop to it. Someone, indeed, was about
to do just that.

While Teresa was dotting the countryside with her
Carmels, the monastery of the Incarnation in Avila —
where she had spent her earlier years of religious life
— was threatened with moral and material ruin.
Religious observance and the quest for perfection
were escaping rapidly through its ever-open parlour
doors, while neglect of finances had brought the nuns
to a state of near destitution and starvation.

View of Segovia, dominated by the Cathedral.

The superiors, namely the Carmelite Provincial, Fr. Angel de Salazar, and the Dominican, Fr. Pedro Fernández, saw the danger of total collapse, but their reaction was to blame Teresa for being the cause of it all... This idea appealed to them, as it gave them an excuse to put a stop to her highly successful founding of reformed monasteries.

With apparent respect, they recalled her and made her prioress of the Incarnation. It was the kind of honour she would gladly have done without, but obediently she embraced this heavy cross and prepared to return to the gilded cage.

On 6 October 1572 she returned to her old monastery, to a community that made no secret of its hostility. The glares and generally threatening behaviour of close on 200 nuns must have stretched her courage to the limit. This hostility stemmed from prejudice against one who had left them to seek greater perfection and their fear that she might now try and convert them all to the discalced way of life. But they need not have feared. With one intuitive stroke of genius, Teresa began to break down the barriers. When she arrived she called them all to the chapter room. There she placed a statue of Our Lady on the prioress's seat and placed her keys beside it, indicating that it was she who would henceforth be prioress. Then she sat on the floor at Our Lady's feet and quietly began to reassure the community with the following words:

"Mothers and sisters, through obedience Our Lord has sent me to this house to perform this duty... I come only to serve you and to please you in any way I can. I am a daughter of this house and the sister of each one of you. Don't be afraid of how I shall govern, because although I have lived and governed among reformed nuns, by God's goodness I am well aware how those who are not should be governed."

In very little time, the great ship of the Incarnation, which had been taking in water at an alarming rate, was again afloat. It had even become a model of

Communion window in the Carmelite convent, Segovia.

Parlour (Carmelite convent, Segovia).

religious life. That it had done so was due in no small measure to its prioress's inspired idea of bringing Fr. John of the Cross as confessor to the community.

This term of office was honourable imprisonment, as we have said, and no matter how honourable it is, a prison is still a prison. The superiors, backed by Rome, saw to it that Teresa could not get out even to attend to pressing problems in monasteries she had founded. Even the Duchess of Alba failed to obtain this permission for her.

But female cunning is a very powerful thing, and when a woman of Teresa's personality and intelligence sets out to achieve something there are no walls or other form of defence capable of stopping her. She appealed directly to King Philip II himself and he granted her request immediately.

She quickly made the journey to Alba, but would neither eat nor sleep at the castle as she had a convent of her own there. She preferred to go up to the castle daily to give this illustrious lady a little of what her fame and riches could not bring her: a little company in the loneliness in which her husband and son, away fighting in Flanders, had left her; and some comfort too in her grief over the love affairs of her son, Don Fadrique.

While she was in Alba she also settled to everyone's satisfaction a quarrel between her daughters and her brother-in-law, Juan de Ovalle, over who should surface a laneway near his house.

She returned to the Incarnation as soon as possible, and from then on the Visitator proved more amenable to further requests to go out.

The nuns in Salamanca took advantage of this improvement to call upon her talent for pouring oil on troubled waters. She went down to them to see if she could succeed in having them moved from the damp and unhealthy house the students had been in to the house which they were trying to buy from that shifty couple, Pedro de la Vanda and his wife.

It was in Salamanca on that occasion that the following incident, as told by herself, happened to her:

Wooden bench used by St. Teresa (Segovia convent).

"One day while I was praying, the Lord told me to go and make a foundation in Segovia. This sounded quite impossible to me, because I couldn't go unless I was told to and the Apostolic Visitator had made it clear that he wanted no more foundations... I wrote and told him that, as he knew, I had been commanded by the Father General to make foundations whenever the opportunity presented itself: that both the bishop and city authorities of Segovia had given permission for one of our monasteries; that I was willing to go ahead with this foundation if ordered to do so... He immediately told me to make this foundation and sent me a licence to do so. I was amazed" (F.21,1-2).

Teresa had had good friends in that ancient Castilian city for some time, particularly a family by the name of Jimena, one of whom had taken the habit in Salamanca. This was Isabel de los Angeles, the nun whose singing of the verse "Would that my eyes could see You..." sent Teresa into ecstasy one Easter morning. She and an aunt and a cousin of hers had often implored Teresa to come and found in Segovia; they had even travelled to Avila to ask her.

Requests, permission, and the word of the Lord convinced Mother Teresa to undertake it, and the hope of being thus enabled to remove her nuns at Pastrana from the vexations of the Princess was an added incentive.

"While still in Salamanca, I arranged to have a house rented for us. I had learned from our experience in Toledo and Valladolid that it was better for many reasons to look for a house of our own after we had

Interior of the Carmelite church (Segovia).

St. Dominic's grotto (in the former Dominican convent in Segovia).

taken possession. In the first place, I didn't have a penny with which to buy a house. Besides, once the monastery was founded, the Lord would provide for it and then a more suitable site could be chosen'' (F.21,2).

Informed by Doña Ana Jimena that all was ready — the permission of Bishop Diego de Covarrubias; permission of the City Fathers, one of whom was a nephew of hers; the house not only rented but furnished as well — Teresa left Salamanca.

First, she went to Avila, via Alba de Tormes and Medina. From there about the middle of March the founding party, consisting of four nuns, Fr. John of the Cross, the chaplain Fr. Julian of Avila, Antonio Gaytán and Mother Teresa herself, set out for Segovia.

Teresa thought it well at this point in her narrative to pause and introduce the last-named member of her party — Antonio Gaytán.

''He was a gentleman who lived in Alba. Some years previously, when he was very much involved in worldly affairs, the Lord had called him... I have said who he was, because in subsequent foundations he worked hard for me and was a great help, so he will be mentioned again. If I were to recount all his virtues, I wouldn't finish so quickly. The virtue that served us best was his mortification; none of the servants who accompanied us saw to our needs as he did. He is a man of great prayer, and the Lord has given him so many graces that circumstances which others would see as obstacles were a pleasure to him and he took them in his stride. All his work for these foundations has been like that. We have been fortunate that the Lord called himself and Fr. Julian of Avila to this work, though Fr. Julian, of course, has been with us from the very beginning. It was through such company as theirs that the Lord must have planned so much good to happen to me. On our journeys they talked of nothing else but God and taught our companions a lot about Him'' (F.21,6).

Then, as if expressing her gratitude to these faithful friends, she adds:

Interior courtyard of the Carmelite convent in Segovia.

St. John of the Cross.

"It is well, daughter, that you who read the story of these foundations should know how indebted we are to them; they work hard without any self-interest so that you can enjoy the blessing of living in these monasteries, and you ought to commend them to the Lord and let them at least have the benefit of your prayers. If you only knew the bad nights and days they went through for you, and the hardships they endured on the roads, you would do this most gladly" (F.21,7).

At last they reached the city of the famous aqueduct, deliberately arriving there after nightfall. It was the evening before the Feast of St. Joseph. They repaired at first to an inn called El Mesón del Aceite and sent word to Doña Ana, who came and took them to their rented house. Everything was so well arranged that Mother Teresa had only to allocate their quarters to everyone and attend to a few minor details.

According to Fr. Julian, "When we arrived we set up an altar and decorated it. Then we hung tapestries on the walls, placed a bell in one of the windows and at dawn I said Mass and reserved the Blessed Sacrament." To that we can add that a notary certified what had taken place and declared the foundation official. It was the Feast of St. Joseph, 19 March 1574, and the monastery was dedicated to St. Joseph of Carmel.

The nuns had three Masses, in fact, that morning. Fr. John of the Cross celebrated the Eucharist when the first Mass was finished, and he had scarcely finished when a visitor arrived. D. Juan de Orozco y Covarrubias, the bishop's nephew and prior of the Canons Regular, happened to be passing by the house. When he saw the porch so clean and decorated he decided to go in and say Mass. This was providential, for he soon proved himself a faithful and obliging friend to the nuns.

Everything had gone very smoothly in this foundation, so smoothly that Mother Teresa was surprised and somewhat puzzled. But her surprise didn't last long. Wherever you go there are always people who envy the success of others. Segovia was no excep-

Overall view of Segovia. In the foreground, the convent of St. John of the Cross.

The fortress at Segovia, opposite the convent of St. John of the Cross.

tion and soon there were people running to the Vicar General to denounce this monastery that had sprung up overnight, complete with altar and bell, nuns and chaplains.

The Vicar General knew nothing of the nuns' arrival, so he hastened indignantly to see for himself. He angrily asked them whose permission they had to do this. The answer that it had been done with the bishop's verbal permission did not satisfy him. He ordered the altar dismantled and the Blessed Sacrament removed. That brought him face to face with the bishop's nephew, who was still saying Mass. The celebrant, however, sang dumb, Fr. Julián hid himself, the nuns were behind their grille, poor Fr. John of the Cross was left to bear the brunt of the attack.

As the high-ranking cleric's anger drew no fire from this saintly little man, and as his anger centred more on their omitting to notify him of their arrival than on the question of permission, it gradually subsided. The

threat of sending them all to jail was reduced to placing a policeman at the door (no one knew exactly what for); and the dismantling of the chapel became a temporary prohibition from reserving the Blessed Sacrament.

Mother Teresa, as usual, remained perfectly calm. As far as she was concerned, it would have been worse if all this had happened before they gained possession. She adapted herself to the law in force at the time. That is why she made these sudden and unexpected strikes when founding monasteries.

As we've already said, the reason why Teresa wanted to have a house in Segovia was to provide a refuge for her long-suffering daughters in Pastrana. It was with this angle in mind that she had brought Julian of Avila and Antonio Gaytán along. Their job was to fetch the nuns from Pastrana, which they did; they had to remove them from their convent by night and their subsequent adventures sounded like something out of a novel.

On the 6th or 7th of April 1574, they finally reached Segovia, their prioress becoming prioress of the new Segovia foundation. That was the end of the Pastrana foundation; it had lasted a bare four years. It was the only one to fail in Teresa's lifetime. Not that she was really surprised at this; with only the whim of a lady for cement, she expected as much from the very first day. Summing it up herself, she said: "In short, the Lord permitted it." No further complaint or ill-feeling. Nor did the Princess hold a grudge against Teresa or her nuns. Perhaps she was no more capable of sustained hatred than she was of steadfast love.... But let us get back to the Segovia house. The day came for moving from a rented house to one of their own. "We stayed there for a few months until a house had been bought, a proceeding which involved us in several lawsuits." (This seems to be an ever present ingredient in Teresa's foundational mix). "We had had considerable trouble of this kind with the Franciscans over a house we were buying nearby. This time it was with the Mercedarians and the Cathedral Chapter.... Oh, Jesus, how troublesome it is to have to contend with such a variety of opinions! Writing about it, it doesn't seem much; but going through it was plenty of trouble" (F.21,9).

The conflicts she is talking about were a common feature of those poor cities: all had numerous religious houses which were dependent on the same sources for their alms.

At last, the house was bought thanks to the influence and money of Doña Ana and her daughter. In fact, both of these ladies were not satisfied with giving the nuns all they had; they both took the habit as well.

The house was in a street quite close to the Cathedral. Too big for its owner, it was nevertheless too small for a community of nuns, especially a strictly enclosed one. They later extended it at the expense of a large part of their garden. All that now remains of the original building are a few "hermitages"; they are really no more than little cells on the second floor, which are now set apart as that floor is no longer used. Saint Teresa used to retire up there for some peace and quiet.

This very fervent community was blessed in having St. John of the Cross's company and teaching during the latter years of his life. When the Discalced Carmelite friars established their headquarters in Segovia and introduced the form of government known as the 'Consulta,' he was the first councillor. So the nuns of Segovia had the benefit of the last teachings of one of the purest and most learned souls the Church ever knew. Two precious letters of his to the two Jimena ladies are still preserved there.

Segovia, then, becomes another point at which these two privileged souls — Teresa and John of the Cross — converged. These twin mystics had a common depth of religious experience; yet they were also very different from one another.

St. John translated his experience into poetry; he sang it and distilled it into verses and symbols. Later, he paraphrased his poems and in doing so produced high-quality theology. For him prayer was life with God, a matter of pure faith and love. He was strongly attracted to ever deeper immersion in the mystery of Christ and to "the feast of the Spirit" which is celebrated in the life of every Christian.

St. Teresa, on the other hand, had so vivid an experience of God that she felt driven to tell people about it. To do so, she needed a group. When she had achieved this she gave it a characteristic lifestyle, "a little college of Christ," she called it. Then, to teach this group she wrote. And in the background there is always the transcendent God, who is at the same time a dear friend and so close that there is no need to shout at Him.

It has been said that Teresa was "water and the thirst for living water," whereas John of the Cross was "fire and waiting for the light in the night." He preferred cosmic symbols: fire, night, mountain, light. She chose more homely ones: garden, water, worm,

Façade of the convent of St. John of the Cross, Segovia.

Tomb of St. John of the Cross, in the Saint's church (Segovia).

butterfly, castle. The fusion of both gave birth to that particular charisma which the Reformed Carmel possessed.

As if grateful to Segovia, St. John of the Cross left it his mortal remains. They were brought there from Ubeda and are venerated in the Friary church which he built. The artistic tomb which contains them is the work of D. Felix Granda.

But our story must go on. Teresa's longest journey to date awaits her, so let us set off once more with her.

91

The start of the foundation of the Carmelite convent in Beas, in the "Book of the Foundations": "Chapter XXII: describes the foundation of the convent of the glorious St. Joseph of the Saviour in the town of Beas, in the year MDLXXV, on the feast of St. Matthias."

Beas de Segura on the map of the Peninsula.

BEAS

St. Teresa's route
from Castile to Andalusia
1575

— October 1574: her term as prioress of the Incarnation convent in Avila having ended, Teresa returned to St. Joseph's carmel.
— late December: Mother Teresa travelled to Valladolid to settle the case of Casilda de Padilla and her relations.
— January 1575: St. Teresa planned a long journey: Valladolid, Medina, Toledo, and Beas (Jaén).
— January 13th: in Medina, Jerónima de la Concepción, Doña Elena de Quiroga's daughter, took the habit at 14 years old. The Saint dedicated verses to her: "Who brought you here maiden / from the valley of sadness? / God and my good fortune."
— February 16th: Teresa arrived at Beas, having crossed the Guadarrama sierra and Despeñaperros pass in the midst of winter.
— February 24th: the Saint founded the carmel at Beas and named Anne of Jesus (Lobera) prioress; she reserved another illustrious nun, María de San José (Salazar), for Seville.
— April: Father Gracián arrived at Beas from Seville, en route for Madrid. Teresa swore obedience to him.

Teresa's distinguished fellows. — The Foundress had now formed a small retinue of illustrious figures around her movement: Fray John of the Cross and Antonio de Jesús (the pioneers from Duruelo), Jerónimo Gracián (the son of the Royal Secretary, the Apostolic Visitator), the Italian Mariano de San Benito (renowned as an engineer), and Juan de Jesús, Roca (a Catalan from Alcalá University). Another Italian, Nicolás Doria, a Genoese financer, was soon to join them. — Teresa had taken the twelve most distinguished nuns of the group with her to Beas: María de San José (prioress of Seville and Lisbon and a great writer) and Anne of Jesus (to whom St. John of the Cross's Spiritual Canticle was addressed, and who later founded Teresian convents in France and Flanders).

Drawing by Hye Hoys (1866-1867): ruins of the Carmelite convent of Beas in the middle of the 19th century. Above, façade of the church.

BEAS DE SEGURA
ST. JOSEPH'S OF THE SAVIOUR
24.2.1575

"While I was still there," writes St. Teresa, referring to her visit to Salamanca to attend to the move to a new house, "a messenger came from Beas (in the Kingdom of Jaén). He brought me letters from a lady of that place and from other people asking me to go and found a monastery there, as they already had a house for the purpose... I questioned the messenger and he told me many good things about the place. And he was right, for it really is very beautiful and has a lovely climate. But when I thought of how far away it was, it seemed foolish to go" (F.22,1).

Indeed, the distance was not the only count on which Beas seemed a folly. Remember, Mother Teresa was in Salamanca as a special favour. Her superiors cannot wait to see her back at the Incarnation, where she was prioress. Moreover, she knew only too well that the Visitator was just as opposed to her looking after

Chiclana.

Overall view of Beas de Segura.

the monasteries already founded as he was to her making any further foundations. Her health, too, was deteriorating and the journey in question was 558 kilometres. After all, Beas was a place she had never heard of; as far as she was concerned it could have have been at the other end of the world; she wondered whether it could still be within the confines of Castile, for she had no permission to found farther afield than that.

But the inner forces driving her to overcome all obstacles were already in motion: her determination to lay down a thousand lives rather than let one soul be lost; her great desire to see one more tabernacle on earth; the thought of how well God would be served in this new house; and, finally, that blind obedience to her Father General who had told her to lose no opportunity of making a new foundation.

If the opportunity was not taken advantage of, it was not going to be her fault; so, she passed the responsibility for a decision on to her superior.

"I thought to myself that since he (the superior) was in Salamanca at the time, I should make no move until I had consulted... When he saw the letters he sent me word that he had been impressed by the devotion of these people and thought they ought not be disappointed. He told me to write and tell them that if they obtained the permission of their Order (Beas belonged to the Knights of Santiago), arrangements would be made for the foundation. He added that they were certain to be refused... but that I should not send them an unfavourable reply" (F.22,3).

So if Teresa was going to play it safe, so was the superior: he didn't refuse, but he was certain nothing would happen. That way he fell foul of neither the lady from Beas nor Mother Teresa.

Who was this lady from Beas? Teresa has answered that herself: "There lived in this town a gentleman called Sancho Rodríguez de Sandoval; he was of noble lineage and well-to-do... Among the children God had given him were two daughters: Doña Catalina Godínez and her younger sister Doña María de Sandoval. The elder of the two would have been fourteen

Impressive close-up of the Despeña-perros Pass, in the heart of the Sierra Morena, the pass from Castile into Andalusia.

(fifteen actually), when the Lord called her to Himself. Until then she had no intention of leaving the world; in fact, she had so high an opinion of herself that her father could not find a suitor who she thought good enough for her'' (F.22,4).

So here was an adolescent with exaggerated expectations; she had her choice of the best bred eligible young men in the kingdom, and they were not good enough. And then the Lord brought about a mysterious change. Her conversion was quite sudden; it happened one day when she read the inscription over the head of the crucified Christ. A simple everyday occurrence like that changed her completely one morning, and the event was accompanied by a mysterious loud noise that woke the whole house up. It must have had something of ''the strong wind'' of Pentecost about it, for then and there Catalina sallied forth in the habit of a *beata* (a woman privately consecrated to God; but not a nun) to let everyone see how determined she was to cut herself off from the world.

The authenticity of the vision was borne out by the change that came over her. She continued to run the house, but also did things which she previously would not have believed herself capable of: like kissing the servants' feet as they lay asleep at night, as if excusing herself for having given them orders during the day; or spending most of the night in prayer since her daytime duties left no time for it.

Four years later, during which time her father died, the Lord tested her with severe illnesses, but these served only to refine her virtue and strengthen her desire to be a nun. They also had the effect of arousing a like desire in her younger sister.

Once their mother was dead, both sisters decided to become nuns; if necessary they would found a monastery of the type they heard Mother Teresa of Jesus was founding. They had heard of these from a Jesuit friend, Fr. Bartolomé de Bustamante. Catalina even had dreams in which she saw herself living in such a community.

There were three apparently insurmountable

obstacles to the fulfilment of these dreams: Catalina's ill-health, which had kept her confined to bed for a number of years past; the licence from the Council of Military Orders, who never granted such licences; the difficulty of communicating with Mother Teresa and getting her to come to Beas when she was being deliberately tied down where she was.

We have seen how the latter difficulty was solved. The first difficulty, too, melted away unexpectedly: on 16 January 1574 Catalina was suddenly and completely cured while a Jesuit celebrated Mass in her room before a picture of Jesus being taken down from the Cross. As for permission from the Knights, it was pointless to even ask them; so Teresa went directly to King Philip II. As soon as he saw the petition was for reformed Carmelites, he immediately granted it.

As Mother Teresa said afterwards: "Lord, it's easily seen that when you want to you easily change anyone's mind!"

She promised the people in Beas that she would be delighted to go as soon as she had made the rounds "of certain monasteries." Her superior was rather annoyed at the turn which events had taken, but he could not refuse the permission he had promised. When her term of office as prioress of the Incarnation had expired, therefore, Teresa began recruiting nuns for the distant foundation she was very soon to embark on.

Leaving Segovia, she visited Avila, Toledo and Malagón. From there she set out with several sisters, the inseparable Fr. Julian and Antonio Gaytán, and a secular priest who was later to become a Discalced Carmelite in Beas, changing his name from Gregorio Martínez to Gregorio Nacianzeno.

Never before had Teresa faced so long a journey, nor had she travelled with so large a party. They left Malagón about the first week in February 1575. In front of them stretched muddy, potholed roads over the never-ending plains of La Mancha. At least the Lord was good enough to bring about a remarkable improvement in Teresa's health, and she had a

Interior of the convent, Beas.

High altar in the nuns' church.

relatively comfortable journey from that point of view. Down they went to Almodóvar del Campo, passing Daimiel and Manzanares on the way. In Almodóvar there is a tradition which presents Teresa as shaking the dust from her sandals over some unpleasantness she experienced there. Whatever about having had an unpleasant experience, the picture of her shaking dust from her sandals is quite far-fetched: she never wore sandals.

In Daimiel there's an equally curious and unlikely tradition. The story goes that Teresa and her party were guests of Don Miguel Merino Morales. He prepared a banquet worthy of his own generosity, and all held their breath to hear the reaction of a saintly stomach to a plate of partridge. Mother Teresa simply tucked in, with the alleged remark "If it's par-

tridge then let it be partridge; if penance, let it be penance."

Behind these stories, which may or may not be true, there is a common desire to show that her holiness was spontaneous, unpretentious, and free of gimmickry; the kind of holiness one would expect of a woman who hated pretence and long faces. The object of the stories is not to show her tolerance of human weakness; but rather, to show the supreme art of making virtue likeable and attractive.

In Almodóvar they stayed with the parents of a man who was later to reform the Trinitarian Order — Bl. John Baptist. From there they crossed into Jaén through Torre de Juan Abad, Villamanrique, etc. and finally reached Beas de Segura.

With lively company, the comments on places more

renowned for bandits than anything else must have been rich. But they don't seem to have experienced any danger worth mentioning; except for an incident near a place called Despeñaperros. They took a wrong turning here and when they realised they were lost, they began to pray to St. Joseph. They immediately heard the voice of an old man warning them to stop or they would find themselves at the bottom of a steep embankment.

Their reception in Beas has been put on record by Fr. Julian of Avila: "The Mother and her nuns were so well received in Beas that... the whole town, young and old alike, turned out to greet them with great rejoicing. Outriders on horseback escorted their wagon to the church grounds, where everyone had gathered to meet them. The clergy, dressed in surplices and led by a cross-bearer, formed a procession, and thus conducted them to the church with all due solemnity. Afterwards, they were taken to the house assigned to them as a monastery and officially received by the lady who had so long desired and sought to have them... We remained with Mother Teresa... until Father Master Jerome Gracián arrived, and then, at his bidding, departed for Seville."

That was 24 February 1575, Feast of St. Matthias. The monastery was called Saint Joseph of the Saviour, and the two Godínez sisters received the Carmelite habit there with every sign of the greatest happiness.

There are two subjects we would like to dwell on before concluding this hurried account of the Beas foundation: the presence here of Fr. Gracián, then at the height of his fame; and the fact that it was here that Teresa fell for the charm of Andalusia.

Although she had heard of Fr. Gracián and had had some correspondence with him, Mother Teresa had never met him until she came to Beas. Son of the famous humanist secretary of King Philip II, Don Diego Gracián de Alderete, and of a mother of Polish origin called Doña Juana Dantisco, Jerome had no fewer than twenty brothers and sisters, all of them quite talented.

CUATRO SIGLOS PASARON
Y TERESA, CAIDA EN ESTOS
VALLES, PISANDO NUESTRAS
CALLES CON SU HUELLA
QUEDARON DEJOS VIVOS
QUE DE ELLA DIMANARON
BEAS 24 - 2 - 1975

The famous frogs' pool (convent garden, Beas), noted for the episode which took place in the time of St. John of the Cross.

St. John of the Cross's altar.

Fr. Jerome himself was an exceptionally gifted man: great personality, unusually retentive memory, fluent orator, fine presence, refined sensibility, and, above all, the tact and patience required to solve interpersonal difficulties.

People far less noble or talented gradually succeeded in turning the Father General against him, especially when he undertook the unenviable task of Visitator to the Carmels (Calced and Discalced) of Andalusia, at the behest of the Dominican Fr. Francisco Vargas. Mother Teresa thought this appointment would enhance the prestige of the Discalced members of the Order; the General, fed much false information, condemned it out of hand.

It was to clarify the true facts of this situation that Fr. Gracían and Mother Teresa met in Beas. Such was the impression he made on her that she described it in words which she had never dared use of anyone else: "I think he's perfect; we couldn't have asked God for better. I have never seen perfection combined with such gentleness. I wouldn't have missed seeing him and speaking with him for anything."

He too has left a record of this meeting: "She revealed her spirit to me without any reservations, and I did likewise with her. We agreed there and then to proceed in complete agreement in all our undertakings. Furthermore, she took a particular vow of obedience to me, over and above her normal religious vow."

What better opportunity than this to take a brief look at that sublime facet of Teresa's soul called friendship?

Friendship for St Teresa is "pure love," something completely disinterested and self-sacrificing. It seeks to provide the beloved with everything good and spare him or her everything harmful. It is enduring in space and time; necessary to the point of being indispensable; open to and complemented by the divine transcendence, for both friends desire the greatest good for one another and the greatest and most lasting good is God.

Teresa saw love and friendship as an absolute and irreplaceable value. Perhaps that is why she looked on God, on her Christ, as a good Friend, and on com-

St. Teresa's cell in the convent, Beas.

munity life as a little group of chosen people in which "all must love one another... all must be friends" (WP.4,7).

She was herself a very winning person and easily aroused love in people around her — her parents, brothers and acquaintances. She had always been particularly gifted in this respect, and the passing years served only to develop it, to increase the radius of its influence.

Her friendships embraced people at all levels of society: cardinals and bishops, priests and religious, bankers and cattle-dealers like Antonio Ruiz who helped her in Malagón, children like Bela and Teresita. Even platonic love had a place in her heart! It is enough to recall the admiration and love she expressed when writing to Fray Luis de Granada, though she knew him only from his writings.

Of all the people her heart went out to, Fr. Gracián was perhaps the object of her greatest friendship. Humanly speaking it was an unlikely friendship — Teresa was sixty at the time, Gracián a mere twenty-eight. But where friendship joins two spirits, age matters little. It was a great pity that so pure a meeting of these kindred spirits presaged a calvary of bitter suffering.

It was all due to a mistake. Teresa had the Prior General's permission to make foundations only in Castile. Neither she nor her advisers had realised that Beas was in Andalusia, as far as ecclesiastical divisions were concerned. To make matters worse, Fr. Gracián thought that once she actually was in Beas he could authorise her to found in Seville, since he was Visitator for Andalusia.

To make a long story short, the Prior General (in Rome) took this as an act of defiance and listened to the calumniators who were portraying both Gracián and Teresa as rebellious troublemakers. Relations between the reformed and the rest of the Carmelite Order became hostile and led to a lot of suffering in the years that followed.

Mother Teresa immediately realised the direction things were taking and hastened to explain herself to the Prior General, but he didn't listen to her. This caused a lot of tension which, being so great a believer in obedience, must have been a very hard moral trial for her indeed.

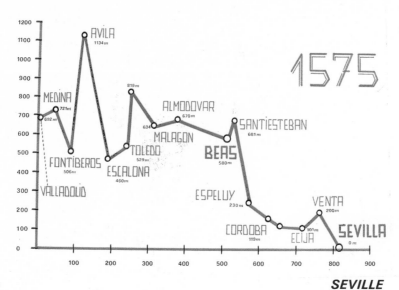

1575

Journey to Seville.

SEVILLE

St. Teresa's route
The Seville adventure

— *April-May 1575: at Beas, Father Gracián ordered the Saint to make a foundation in Seville.*
— *May 18th: Teresa began the journey from Beas to Seville via Córdoba.*
— *May 23rd: she arrived in Córdoba and entered the city with difficulties. Mass at the little Campo de la Verdad church.*
— *May 24th (Whitsun week): the Saint received further intimate graces, at St. Anne's hermitage in Ecija.*
— *May 26th: she arrived in Seville.*
— *May 29th: foundation of the Seville convent.*
— *August 12th: Mother Teresa's brothers arrived at Sanlúcar de Barrameda, from America.*
— *November 24th: the Saint planned the foundation at Caravaca, which was achieved the following month.*
— *May 27th 1576: she moved to the new Seville carmel.*
— *the following day, May 28th, the Saint set out from Seville for Castile.*
— *June 23rd: she arrived in Toledo. It had been decided that she should suspend her founding work.*

Tried by the Inquisition. — *A combination of accusations: the* Book of her Life *was denounced in Castile; Teresa and her nuns were accused in Seville. Don Alvaro de Mendoza handed the manuscript of the Saint's book over to the Castilian Inquisitors. The renowned Dominican theologian Domingo Báñez defended it before the court (July 7th 1575); but Teresa's work was to continue in the Inquisitors' prison. In Seville the Inquisitors interrogated Mother Teresa, who dispelled their suspicions with ease; but she had to write two long* Relations *about her life and mystical experiences (Relations 4 & 5).*

Account of the foundation of Seville from the "Book of the Foundations": "Chapter XXIII: deals with the foundation of the convent of the glorious St. Joseph of Carmel in the city of Seville. The first Mass was celebrated on the feast of the Holy Trinity in the year MDLXXV."

Façade of the present Carmelite convent in Seville.
Drawing by Hye Hoys (1866-1867).

SEVILLE
ST. JOSEPH OF SEVILLE
29.5.1575.

"The older she gets, the more she travels," moaned
Fr. Julian on one occasion; and how right he was.

When she was younger, Mother Teresa did not look
beyond the immediate vicinity of Avila for oppor-
tunities to found; now that she is old and plagued by
persistent bad health her journeys get longer and
longer.

This time the target was Seville. God knows it was
not of her own choosing; her reason and the Lord
Himself told her that this move would mean plenty of
trouble, and had she been free to choose she would
have preferred Caravaca or Madrid. In fact she had
already chosen nuns for the latter. But Fr. Gracián,
who was now her immediate superior, had other
ideas and so she penetrated more deeply into Andalusia.

There was a certain sadness about her departure from
Beas; she had a presentiment that she would never be

Part of the city, with the Giralda in the foreground.

with these sisters again. When she was leaving she said to the prioress, Mother Anne: "Here, take my mantle! It's new and more suitable for a young person like you. I'll take yours; it's old and worn, so it will suit me fine."

And so she took her leave of this monastery which, through St. John of the Cross's lavish attentions, was later to become a nursery of some famous foundresses. On Friday, 20 May, the party set out — she took six nuns, as well as Julian of Avila, Antonio Gaytán, Fr. Gregorio Nacianzeno and a retinue of drivers and mule boys. Teresa had a very high opinion of these six sisters: "They were such that I would have dared to go even to the land of the Turks with

them... They had a long way to go, so I made sure they were the most suitable for our purpose" (F.24,6).

The caravan consisted of four covered wagons, their luggage being minimal. Father Mariano had been instructed to have everything ready for them in Seville, and had painted a very rosy picture of what they would find there; so why bother to bring any more than they needed for the journey? They did bring food, but the heat soon made that inedible; fortunately, Mother Teresa also insisted on a supply of water.

This journey turned out to be Teresa's longest and most adventurous. All sorts of things happened to

them — some funny, others far from it. Let us listen to the accounts which the travellers themselves have left us:

"For all our hurry we didn't reach Seville till the Thursday before Trinity Sunday (26 May), and we suffered from the most intense heat on the way. We didn't travel during siesta time, and yet, sisters, getting into those wagons was like going to Purgatory, for the sun had been beating down on them. Sometimes by thinking of Hell and others by telling themselves they were doing or suffering something for God, those sisters bore the journey happily and cheerfully" (F.24,6).

The first day they took their siesta in a pleasant forest. Such was the profusion of water, flowers and birds that Mother Teresa became enraptured and they had difficulty moving her from the place. That was only the honeymoon.

They spent the first night at a hermitage dedicated to St. Andrew, situated a short distance beyond Santistéban. They alternated between praying and resting on the cold stone floor.

In the cool dawn they moved on towards Linares, fording two rivers on the way. At midday, Fr. Julian tells us, "We came to an inn by the roadside. There were some men there, and I had never seen such a depraved lot in all my life... They shouted all sorts of vile things at Fr. Gregorio Nacianzeno and there was no way we could prevail on them to stop it... In the end, they drew knives and began fighting among themselves... While all this was going on the Mother and sisters remained in their covered wagons, and were not seen. Had the men seen them, they would have treated them as they had treated Father Gregorio."

And as if that were not enough, he adds: "We were very thirsty in this inn... The heat was unbearable; a cup of water cost two maravedís, and each sister needed several. Wine was cheaper than water there."

As for food, María de San José tells us that "most days there were only beans, bread, cherries and

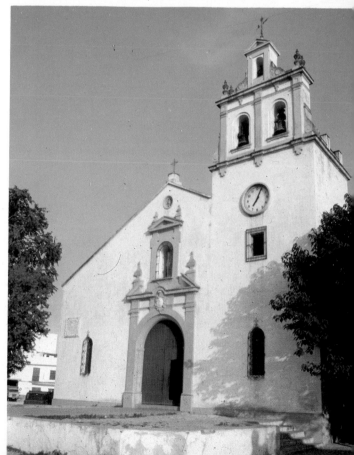

Ruins of the "Venta de Albino," near Carmona.

Interior of the Cathedral (Mosque) of Córdoba. ▷

which could have cost us very dear." What happened was that one of the wagons broke loose and drifted downstream, nuns and all. Some of the remaining nuns were immediately on their knees crying out to God, while others helped the men to haul on a rope. Fortunately, the prayers were heard and the wagon became grounded on a sandbank. A gentleman who had been watching the proceedings helped them get on their way again.

The third day, with no worse enemy than the unrelenting sun to contend with, they made good progress through Villanueva, Argonilla, Pedro Abad and El Carpio, a pretty little hamlet of some 250 souls.

The fourth day was undoubtedly the worst. Mother Teresa became so ill that they had to seek refuge in an inn. According to Fr. Julian, "They were given a little room in which pigs used to be kept." As described by Teresa, "The little room was roofed like a shed and had no windows. If you opened the door the sun blazed in. The sun here is not like in Castile; it is much worse. They put me to bed, but I would have been better off on the floor for the bed was so uneven that I didn't know what way to lie; it was like a bed of sharp stones" (F.24,8). María de San José had a few further remarks to make about this incident: "That was all she (Teresa) noticed; she didn't see all the cabinets and bugs... But that is what happened... And then there was the shouting and swearing of the people... and the noise of the dancing and tambourines. In the end we decided it was better to take her out of there, so we set off again in the full fury of the early afternoon sun."

That night they slept near an inn just outside Córdoba, rather than face the uproar of an inn.

The fifth day was Pentecost Sunday, 22 May, and it began early in Córdoba. Teresa tells us about that morning: "I found what happened on Pentecost Sunday harder to bear than the things I've mentioned

things like that. If we found an egg for our Mother we thought it a great thing."

They passed Linares and Alventoso (scene of a famous battle with the Moors) and reached the ferry where one crossed the Guadalquivir. Here, more adventure. Fr. Julian writes: "The boatman cheated us; he said his boat would take us all, but it was fit for only a small number of people and horses. For the sake of a little extra profit he tried to do something

Calle de la Pimienta, in the Santa Cruz quarter.

above. We tried to get into Córdoba as early as we could so that we could hear Mass without being seen. We were directed to a church just over the bridge, for greater privacy. But when we went to cross the bridge, we found that the wagons couldn't cross without a licence from the governor. Since people were not yet up, it took over two hours to obtain that, and meanwhile a lot of people began to gather trying to find out who were in the wagons... When the licence came, the wagons were found to be too wide to go through the bridge gate. They (the projecting ends of the axles, actually) had to be sawn, and that took more time. When we finally got to the church it was full of people, being the church of the Holy Spirit... so there was a solemn celebration and a sermon...

We alighted near the church. Nobody could see our faces because we had our veils down, but the sight of us like that and with our white mantles... and *alpargatas* (rope-soled canvas shoes) was enough to cause an uproar... As we entered the church a man came up to me and held back the people. I begged him to show us to a side chapel; he did so and closed the door on us. He did not leave us until he had seen us safely out of the church...

You may think this was nothing, sisters, but I assure you it was one of the worst things I've been through in my life. From the uproar in the congregation one would have thought the church had been invaded by bulls'' (F.24,12-14).

The sixth day brought them to the relatively large town of Ecija (7,000 inhabitants). Here they were unmolested as they attended Mass and received the sacraments at their leisure in the hermitage of St. Anne. Mother Teresa spent the day shut away in the sacristy thanking the Holy Spirit for his favours. That day, too, she made a special vow of obedience to Fr. Gracián for life.

They were now only fifteen leagues from Seville. They still had to pass through Fuentes and the

Carmona, entry into the town.

The old "calle de Armas" (Alfonso XII), site of the first house occupied by the Saint and her group in Seville.

The "calle de Armas."

somewhat frightening incident at the inn of Andino. What happened at the said inn is told by Sister Leonor de San Gabriel: "Near an inn they call Andino Inn, we came on a group of soldiers and muleteers fighting with knives. There was complete disorder and nobody could make them stop. Mother (Teresa) stuck her head out of the wagon and with one word calmed them all down."

The last night was spent at Mairena, a pretty, white little town with fountains. Then, at dawn they heard Mass and were on their way to the promised land.

In those days Seville had, without a doubt, the highest population of any city in Spain. With some 30,000 permanent residents and a considerable floating population, being the point of departure for all Spanish American traffic, it was at the height of its fame and splendour. As Port of the Indies it was a clearing house for dreamers of adventure and, being also the gateway through which Spain's riches entered and were distributed, it was a mecca for the big merchants, for soldiers, priests, missionaries, as well as every conceivable kind of rogue.

The Church in Seville was presided over by Don Cristóbal de Rojas y Sandoval, a great friend of Fr. Gracián's and of Discaced Carmelites generally. He had given them the much coveted hermitage of Los Remedios, and longed to see Mother Teresa, whom he knew only from their correspondence.

As well as having possibly the finest Cathedral in Spain, Seville had no fewer than thirty parishes as well as numerous chapels. Besides, there were eighteen houses of friars and twenty-four convents in it.

This, then, is the Seville which Teresa's four covered wagons entered on the morning of Thursday, 26 May 1575. Frs. Gracián and Mariano had painted such a pretty picture of how things would be that Teresa thought she would rest for a few days and then return to Castile.

There was no need to worry about the house; Fr. Mariano had already rented one. They were bound to

*View of "Los Remedios" beyond the Guadalquivir,
convent of Discalced Carmelite friars where St. Teresa
was received.*

be well provided for financially in a city of so much wealth. The usual difficulty in obtaining episcopal permission did not arise — nobody even mentioned it — because the archbishop was more like a father to them and was eagerly looking forward to meeting Mother Teresa. Fr. Gracián even had young ladies already waiting to join the community.

But when reality hit them, it was like waking up out of a beautiful dream. "Harsh reality" we say, and that it was.

They considered the house "small and damp." It was furnished, but they found that all the furniture had only been lent for their arrival and most of it was reclaimed almost immediately. With no friends or acquaintances to call to their assistance, the money pro-

vided by Fr. Mariano didn't go very far. And to crown everything, nobody had bothered to mention, or had apparently noticed, that the archbishop was totally opposed to monasteries founded in poverty. What he had been looking forward to was having Teresa and her nuns help him reform the convents of Seville!

That in itself might have been reason enough to return to Castile without making any foundation, but there was worse to come. Tension was high between the Discalced and their brethren of the Ancient Observance — now called Calced Carmelites. There was internal trouble too: in spite of Teresa's care in the selection of suitable nuns for this arduous undertaking, she let one bad egg slip into the basket. After giving untold trouble she finally left the Order, but only to continue her mischief-making: her lies and false testimonies brought the Inquisition down on Mother Teresa. It had been keeping tabs on her for a while back, and now decided to hold an inquiry into the life her nuns led and into everything concerning herself.

Whenever Fr. Gracián bemoaned this intrusion or the Inquisition's investigation of her *Life,* Teresa would only laugh and say: "I wish they burned us all at the

"White mantle" used by St. Teresa (among the relics kept in the convent in Seville).

stake for Christ. But don't be afraid, Father; where matters of faith are concerned, by God's goodness, they will find nothing wrong with us; we would prefer to die a thousand deaths."

The first few months of her stay in Seville were indeed difficult ones for Teresa. So much so that at times her renowned courage failed her.

"No one could have foreseen," she confesses, "that in a wealthy city so full of rich people there would be less help forthcoming for a foundation than in any place I've been. I don't know if it's the climate of those parts. I've always heard it said that the devil has a freer hand there for tempting people, and I was certainly sorely pressed by him. I have never seen myself so weak and cowardly in all my life as I was there" (F.25,1).

Nevertheless, the Lord gradually undid the knots in which they were so terribly tied up.

After several petitions from Fr. Mariano, the archbishop allowed Mass to be said in the house on Trinity Sunday, 29 May, provided they avoided solemnity. After that he frequently sent one of his chaplains to say Mass for them and to enquire after Mother Teresa. Finally he paid them a visit himself and, as Teresa wrote to Antonio Gaytán, "he did what I wanted." So much did the archbishop change, in fact, that he subsequently gave them wheat, money and other gifts, and also showed many signs of real respect for them.

Outstanding benefactors now began to come forward. The names of people like Doña Leonor de Varela, a cleric called Garciálvarez, the saintly prior of the nearby Carthusians, etc. will always have a place in accounts of the founding of this monastery.

The sky was completely cleared of its threatening clouds with the longed-for arrival of Teresa's brother Lorenzo from America. At his own expense he undertook to solve the last of their problems: the purchase of a house.

Lorenzo was Teresa's favourite brother. He had been several years in Ecuador and had done very well for

Drum and sticks, a memento of the Saint's very human gaiety (in the convent in Seville).

House in the "calle de la Pajería" where St. Teresa set up her foundation.

Drum and sticks, a memento of the Saint's very human gaiety (in the convent in Seville).

House in the "calle de la Pajería" where St. Teresa set up her foundation.

himself, rising to the post of Mayor of Quito. He had sent her money on several occasions previously, even for her very first house in Avila. Now he was home, with his children — Francisco, Lorenzo and Teresita. His brother, Don Pedro de Alumada, had come with him too, but a third brother, Jerónimo de Cepeda, had died in Panama shortly before they were due to embark.

What a joy it must have been for Teresa to embrace her loved ones after so many years, and to see her nephews and the pretty nine-year-old Teresita for the first time. Her charming little niece was to provide her with many pleasurable moments in these latter years of her life. If we may anticipate a little, it was when she was on her way from Burgos to Avila to receive Teresita's profession that Teresa died in Alba de Tormes.

How often Teresa had dreamed of America! That was where all her brothers were, and she kept in constant touch with them. Now, most of them were dead.

America had made an impression on Teresa in several ways. The millions of souls who were outside the Church, those "Indians" she kept hearing about — tales of civilization and evangelization; tales too of exploitation. "Those Indians cost me dearly," she once wrote in a letter to Lorenzo. America conjured up too the new image of the world — how much more immense creation was than anyone had ever thought!

America occupies a much larger place in her books and her whole outlook than it does in those of John of the Cross. Yet the latter died just when he was being sent to Mexico. Some people would have liked to send Teresa to Mexico too; not her superiors, but the evil tongues of mischief-makers in Andalusia.

Everything that came from America enthralled Teresa. Potatoes, which were to do so much to alleviate hunger in Europe, native medicines with enchanting names, and above all, coconuts. When they sent her one from Seville to Toledo, trying to get it open turned into quite a community event.

Proof of the impact which the New World made on

Teresa is extant in the form of various objects from it which are still cherished in her Carmels, especially in Avila and Seville.

When all the initial opposition and trials were over, the people of Seville quickly came to love both Teresa and her daughters. Vocations flourished and in her spare moments she loved to watch the royal fleet in the port, where there were always ships sailing for or returning from America.

Teresa believed in "thinking big" and aiming high. Her thoughts took her to Europe as well as America — the wars in Flanders and Portugal, the widespread religious strife, etc.

But to turn to something more pleasant, the Discalced nuns had a house of their own at last. It was situated in the Calle de Zaragoza, in the parish of St. Mary Major, close to the magnificent Franciscan monastery. Today the City Hall stands in its place.

The new monastery was inaugurated and blessed on 3 June 1576, and dedicated to St. Joseph of Seville. The occasion followed the usual pattern of Mass, procession and general rejoicing. The archibishop reserved the Blessed Sacrament and then, at her own request, publicly blessed Mother Teresa. To her consternation, however, the archbishop — who appreciated her spiritual stature more than most — then insisted on her blessing him, in public. Though considerably embarrassed, she complied with his request.

We cannot end our account of Seville without mentioning that the two most faithful portraits of St. Teresa — one a painting, the other a word picture — date from this time.

The first was made by a brother whom we have already met at Pastrana, Fray Juan de la Miseria. Fr. Gracián commissioned it, and it shows more goodwill than artistic merit. Teresa agreed to sit for it only under obedience. The story goes that when it was finished, she said: "God forgive you, Brother John, but you've certainly made me look ugly and bleary-eyed."

The second is the expression of a complete knowledge of the Saint drawn with love and reverence and enshrined in the following beautiful lines by María de San José:

"This Saint was of average height, maybe a little more. In her youth she had the name of being very beautiful, and one could see to the very end that she really was. Her face was rather unusual, being neither round nor oval; her forehead was high, smooth and very beautiful; her eyebrows, auburn rather than black, were wide and a little arched; her brown eyes were round and sparkling; they were not very large, but they were very well set. Her straight nose narrowed towards the top, and neatly met the eyebrows, forming a pleasing bridge between them. The top of the nose was round and flattened a little. The nostrils were small and arched. The nose as a whole did not protrude very much from her face... Her mouth was well-proportioned, the upper lip straight and thin, the lower thicker and slightly protruding. It was a graceful and prettily coloured mouth....

On the whole, she was more inclined to be stout than thin, but very well-proportioned. She had small but lovely hands. On the left side of her face there were three moles, like little warts, rising in a line from just below the left side of her mouth."

Very soon all that Seville would retain of St. Teresa would be these two portraits and a host of precious memories.

Once she had seen her daughters safely ensconced in their new home, she bade them farewell on 4 June 1576. Ten years later, thanks to the generosity of Don Pedro Cerezo Pardo, they moved to the monastery they have occupied ever since. This benefactor's only daughter entered the Order in 1618 and brought with her Teresa's most famous work, *The Interior Castle* — Fr. Gracián had given her father a present of it.

Today this book, protected by an artistic reliquary, is the community's most prized possession. Other relics or memorabilia still preserved here include: a substantial collection of letters; a joint of her little finger; a

white mantle worn by the Saint; one of her *alpargatas;* Fray Juan's portrait of her; and various other objects connected with her.

What remains, above all, is Teresa's cheerfulness. Her charm and wit have fused with those of the Andalusian temperament to make of this community a worthy witness to the woman for whom "a sad saint was a sad sort of saint."

Embossed silver cover which for several centuries bound the Autograph of the "Interior Castle" (Seville - Carmelite convent).

Reliquary in silver and crystal, a symbol of the "Interior Castle." It contains the Autograph of the book.

Autograph of the "Interior Castle" (Carmelite convent - Seville).

Portrait of Mother Teresa (at the age of sixty), by the Italian painter fray Juan de la Miseria (Carmelite convent - Seville).

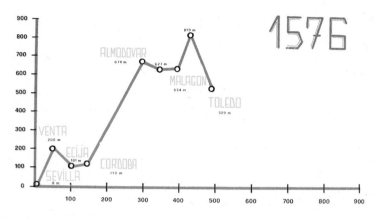

1576

The Saint's route on her way back to Castile.

Foundation of Caravaca from the "Book of the Foundations": "Chapter XXVII: describes the foundation in the town of Caravaca. The Blessed Sacrament was reserved on New Year's Day, MDLXXVI. It is dedicated to the glorious St. Joseph."

CARAVACA

St. Teresa's route
A foundation from a distance

— March 1575: the Saint sent two deputies, Julian of Avila and Antonio Gaytán, to Caravaca to negotiate the foundation.
— June 9th 1575: the king took steps to avoid obstacles for the foundation.
— July 19th: the Saint wrote thanking King Philip for the aforementioned resolution.
— November 24th-25th: St. Teresa and Fr. Gracián granted authorisation to the founders.
— December 18th: the founders' caravan arrived at the town of Caravaca.
— January 1st 1576: foundation of the Caravaca convent. The Saint had sent Ana de San Alberto (later a distinguished disciple of St. John of the Cross) as prioress.

Historical background.
— These were five or six turbulent years for Mother Teresa: 1575-1581. — The General Chapter, in Piacenza (Italy), declared opposition to her work (1575). In Seville she received notification that she was sentenced to seclusion, with threats of excommunication. — Fr. John of the Cross was arrested and imprisoned in Avila. — A new Papal Nuncio, Felipe Sega, came from Rome to Madrid: he condemned Gracián and declared the Saint to be "a restless gadabout of a woman, disobedient and obstinate." — At the same time, the Inquisition seized Teresa's most important book, her Life, and observed closely the Mother's activities and behaviour. — It was with this background that she travelled from Seville to Toledo (1576) and from Toledo to Avila (1577). — And with this stormy background she wrote her masterpiece, The Interior Castle (Toledo-Avila, 1577). — The outcome was eventually favourable: in March 1581 Teresa's family was to obtain its autonomy, with its own superiors and laws.

Façade of the Carmelite convent in Caravaca: drawing by Hye Hoys (1866-1867).

CARAVACA
ST. JOSEPH'S MONASTERY
1.1.1576

This is a very old town; Ptolemy referred to it as Carca, and it later became Caravaca. Under Arab rule

Caravaca was in the Kingdom of Todmir; at a later stage it even had a king of its own. After it had been taken back from the Moors, it was donated to an uncle of King James I; then it passed into the hands of the Knights Templar, and belonged in Teresa's time to the Order of Santiago.

To quote Alcázar, "It is situated on a pleasant plain, has good walls, old-style towers, and is dominated by a strong castle. The surrounding countryside is fertile in bread, wine, olive oil, honey, fruit, silk, and hemp, as well as being good for cattle and hunting. It has a population of about 600 people."

A small number of these people played a prominent role in our story: D. Alonso Muñoz, a member of the Council for the Indies, and his wife Doña Catalina de

Santa Cruz fortress/sanctuary in Caravaca.

Otalora; Don Rodrigo Moya and his wife Doña Elvira Caxa.

It so happened that Doña Catalina lost her husband, and shortly afterwards three high-born young maidens (all related to one another) left church one day, after hearing a sermon by a Jesuit, determined to leave the world and enter a convent. All three were called Francisca: their surnames being de Saojosa, de Cuéllar, and de Tauste. Since the first was a niece of Doña Catalina's and the second a daughter of her friend Sr. de Moya, Doña Catalina agreed to have all three come to live with her. Caravaca had no convent so she promised to help them found one, and, on the advice of the Jesuit Fathers, they decided to invite Mother Teresa of Jesus to advise them on founding the kind of monastery she was founding.

Mother Teresa received this invitation when she was in Avila. She has told us herself how it affected her: "When I saw the desire and the fervour of those good people and considered how far afield they had to go in search of Our Lady's Order, I was quite moved and I wanted to help them realize their good intention. I was told the place was near Beas, so I took more nuns with me than I would otherwise have done... with the intention of going on to Caravaca when the Beas monastery had been founded. But as the Lord had decided otherwise, my plans were of little use, as I've said when speaking of Seville" (F.27,2).

Views of the town and convent, Caravaca.

When Mother Teresa reached Beas she found out that Caravaca was not as near as she had thought. She was also told that the roads were impassable. In that case, she reasoned, confessors and supervisors would have considerable difficulty visiting the sisters. And that somewhat cooled her enthusiasm. Still, she had given her word; so she sent Fr. Julian of Avila and Antonio Gaytán off on a fact-finding mission.

The two men set off across what is now the province of Albacete to that of Murcia, where Caravaca was. They were guests of Don Rodrigo Moya, Francisca de Cuéllar's father, during their stay. One of the girls had changed her mind in the meantime, and Doña Catalina did not have enough money for the project, but the impression made on the two emissaries was such that the necessary papers for the foundation were signed before they left.

"They left the ladies very happy, and returned well pleased with both ladies and the place itself... though not so pleased with the roads" (F.27,4).

With the agreement drawn up, one end of the business had been brought to a satisfactory conclusion. There was, however, another end still to be tied up, so to speak: the permission of the Military Order of Santiago. This time the problem was a little different from that encountered in Beas. The Knights were willing to authorise the foundation, but on condition that the nuns would become subject to them; and Teresa was not going to have that.

The great social and political influence which these half monastic, half military institutions wielded in 16th-century Spain was one of the lingering vestiges of the Middle Ages. St. Teresa was certainly not going to allow her nuns to become the subjects of such people. Faithful to her Order, she was determined that whatever she founded was going to be under obedience to the General, for the said General, Juan Bautista Rubeo, had clearly requested her to found "within the Carmelite Order."

Statue of Our Lady, sent by the Saint to the convent in Caravaca.

Statue of St. Joseph, dating from the Saint's time (Carmelite convent - Caravaca).

In confirmation of that, we might mention in passing that she was offered a foundation in Valencia about this time by the archbishop himself. But she refused because he made it a condition that the house be subject to himself.

Ironically, while Teresa was doing her utmost to be loyal to the General, he and the General Chapter had just condemned her. She was ordered to cease all founding activity and to retire to a monastery — it was a form of "house arrest."

However, she did not know of that decision yet, and her reaction to the obstacle placed in her way by the Knights was to appeal, as she always did in such emergencies, to the King himself.

Philip II settled the matter quickly. He made an exception for her, but added that the nuns were to pay tithes to the Order of Santiago and acknowledge its right to give permission. With the control of the Knights reduced to certain monetary matters, Teresa was happy and wrote once more to thank the King. Once more, too, she urged her daughters not to tire of praying for him.

This was not the first letter Teresa wrote to the King, as we have already seen; nor would it be the last. He was her court of appeal in all serious issues. Thus she wrote asking his support when she wanted the Discalced to become a separate province within the Carmelite Order. She wrote to defend Fr. Gracián when he was defamed and persecuted. She called on him for justice when Fr. John of the Cross was imprisoned in the Toledo priory. This latter, indeed, was perhaps the strongest and most daring letter she ever wrote.

We have alluded several times to certain "tensions among the friars." As we shall have to do so again, it may be no harm to quote some lines from the considered judgement of that great historian of Carmel, Fr. Silverio:

"As always happens in such cases, the reformation which Teresa so opportunely undertook was evaluated quite differently by different people at first. They were not to know the fruit which it would, in time, bear in the Church. It is not surprising, therefore, that the Calced Fathers should have had some misgivings about it and even opposed it. Apart from some excesses, which are inevitable whenever feelings run high, Calced and Discalced proceeded with the best of intentions, and God availed of the struggle between them to purify the virtue of their holy Foundress and make the Reform more vigorous. When the long and exhausting storm was over, the Reform came out of it strong and buoyant. Calmly evaluating those events today, it is easy to excuse both sides for what they did."

But, to return to Caravaca. By the time the problem of the licence, or permission, had been solved, Teresa was on her way to Seville. She and Fr. Gracián agreed that as she could not go personally, the nuns would have to make the journey without her. They were accompanied by two Discalced Fathers and the faithful Fr. Julian and Antonio Gaytán.

So, for once, Teresa had to write of what she heard rather than what she saw: "When they arrived, the people received them with great joy, especially those who were already enclosed. They founded the monastery and reserved the Blessed Sacrament on the Feast of the Holy Name of Jesus (1 January)

1576. Immediately afterwards, both girls took the habit" (F,27,9). The monastery was dedicated to St. Joseph.

It was the first time a nun other than St. Teresa — Sr. Ana de San Alberto from Malagón — took charge of a foundation. Teresa would never see Caravaca, in fact, but it had a special place in her heart. It was also one of St. John of the Cross's favourite communities. He visited it several times, and it is one of the few Carmels that have preserved the letters he wrote them.

The town of Caravaca still proudly displays Teresa's original agreement in its Municipal Archive.

One curious little sign of Teresa's affection for the Caravaca Carmel and, indeed, for the traditions of the town, is the devotion she displayed from then onwards for their famous relic of the true Cross, better known as the Caravaca Cross. She carried a reproduction of it about with her for the rest of her life and it was found between the sheets of her death bed when the body was removed.

This curious fact deserves a few words on Teresa's love of symbols such as this. She was always a lover of images and symbols.

Her faith in such things — in this case the Caravaca Cross — was not in any sense a kind of fetishism. They were concrete representations of a mystery, and her use of them was not a latching on to something superficial, but a reminder of something profoundly religious.

It's a pity we cannot indulge ourselves here in a proper consideration of Teresa's use of symbols. But we cannot pass up the opportunity of saying something, however brief, about it.

Take, for example, her approach to Christ. Even here her symbolist approach is in evidence, whether in the form of the Cross or the marriage symbols of the Song of Songs.

And there is the way she understands the soul as a

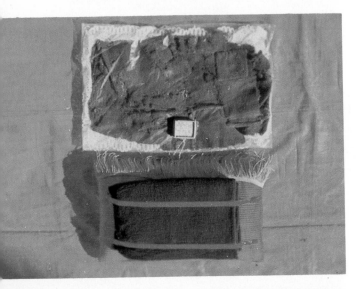

Autograph of St. John of the Cross.

The Saint's scapular.

The choir in the convent.

castle and as a garden. It was as if she bore within herself simultaneously the strength suggested by the one and the fertility of the other.

Life itself, especially that of the spirit, is perceived in terms of two beautiful symbols: the silkworm destined to be transformed into a butterfly; and water, springing from the foot of the rock and giving life to all it touches, or that which wells up in the inner fountain of the soul and flows through every human action into every undertaking.

And, finally, for the sake of brevity, the symbolic mystery, which she made so much her own, of the struggle between water and fire. The water she receives from Christ; the fire she has within herself — "great desires" and the inner drive to do more and more.

Teresa thought of such things as these when she held her little Caravaca Cross. According to tradition, this Cross had its origin in a vision which the slave priest Ginés Pérez had in the days of the Arab domination. Later, as an artifact, this cross is alleged to have converted the Moorish petty king Abu Zeit. In the end the Cross was stolen and what Caravaca treasured in Teresa's time was a relic of the True Cross, which had been sent by the Pope to comfort the townsfolk on the loss of their treasure.

Cross of Caravaca.

la fun da Tio de my ng lla sun ba de la faia

*P̃ d caba da la fun da Tio de fe d lla ca faio los fun da gones
por nos de quatro nios faca 9 fa fue y começa io gran de per
fe cu gio nes mun de gol pe a los des calcos y des cal ços q̃ ã q̃ ya*

Account of the foundation in the "Book of the
Foundations": "The foundation in Villanueva de la Jara.
After the foundation in Seville was finished, there were
no more foundations for four years. The reason for this
was the beginning of sudden tremendous persecution
against the...."

Villanueva de la Jara (Cuenca), on the map of the
Peninsula.

VILLANUEVA DE LA JARA

St. Teresa's route
in the lands of Don Quixote
1580

— June 25th 1579: St Teresa travelled to Medina and
  Valladolid.
— June 30th 1579: further journeys from Valladolid to
  Medina, Alba and Salamanca.
— November 1579: the Saint set out from Salamanca to
  Avila; from there she travelled to Toledo and then
  Malagón, wheré she arrived on November 24th, and
  directed building work on the new convent.
— February 13th 1580: Teresa left Malagón, accompanied
  by the founding nuns. She paused (17th-19th) at Roda,
  the Socorro hermitage, where the venerable Catalina de
  Cardona had lived.
— February 21st: arrival at Villanueva de la Jara.
— February 25th: she gave the founders their habits.
— March 18th: the Saint injured her left arm again, with
  the winch of the well. She had first dislocated it in Avila
  on December 24th 1577.
— March 20th: Mother Teresa left Villanueva de la Jara for
  Toledo: on arrival on the 26th she was seriously ill.
— June 7th-8th: she travelled from Toledo to Madrid and
  then Segovia, arriving on the 13th.
— July 6th: from Segovia to Avila.
— early August: from Avila to Medina and Valladolid,
  where she fell seriously ill with the famous "universal
  cold."

Historical background.
— Teresa: *her health was now extremely delicate. She suffered once again from problems with her left arm, which
  had been out of action for several months in 1578. She
  fell ill at the end of the journey back to Toledo; and
  caught the summer epidemic which ravaged Castile that
  year. As a result her strength was severely reduced.*
— Her work *and the group of followers: the storm was
  blowing over; the foundations recommenced. On May
  5th, Fr. Gracián was reinstated to his honour and duties.
  Juan Bautista Caffardo was elected as the Order's new
  Prior General on May 21st. On June 22nd it was decided, in Rome, to grant the status of autonomous province to Mother Teresa's friars and nuns ("Pia Con-
  sideratione" brief).*
— Political situation: *King Henry of Portugal had died:
  Philip II claimed his right to the throne, but Don Antonio
  was proclaimed king in Lisbon. War ensued; the Duke of
  Alba invaded the kingdom. The Saint wrote a distressed
  letter "against war" to Don Teutonio de Braganza (July
  22nd 1579).*

Exterior of the Carmelite convent in Villanueva de la Jara: drawing by Hye Hoys (1866-1867).

VILLANUEVA DE LA JARA
ST. ANNE'S MONASTERY
21.2.1580

"With the founding of the Seville monastery (which came after Caravaca, though it is described before it)

there were no more foundations for over four years. This was because of the great persecution to which both male and female Discalced were suddenly subjected. There had been some before of course, but never as bad as this; it almost put an end to the whole undertaking. It showed clearly how the devil felt about the holy beginning the Lord had accomplished, and that it was really His work, for it had made considerable progress. The Fathers, especially their leaders, suffered greatly from the almost total opposition of the Calced Fathers" (F.28,1).

Marvellous how calmly and briefly St. Teresa dismisses this truly bitter parenthesis!

The forces of this female "conquistador" had been confined to barracks until further notice. Her energies, however, would grow on the memory of

Overall view of Villanueva de la Jara.

what had been accomplished and turn for the moment to inner growth and consolidation.

She was not ordered to retire to any monastery in particular, but the one she chose was Toledo. Perhaps her friendship with the Post Master of the city prompted her to do this, because for the foreseeable future she was going to have to conduct all her business by post. Or it may have been the pleasant climate, so beneficial to her poor state of health, which attracted her.

Most of her time in Toledo was devoted to writing: a torrent of letters, the continuation of the *Mansions* and *Foundations,* a little work called "How to make a visitation of Discalced Carmelite monasteries," etc.

She also dreamed. She relived those beautiful days in her first foundation ("the most restful of her life"), and the interminable travels that followed. While she is in forced retirement, let us too take a closer look at those travels.

Like St. Paul, Teresa was one day impelled by the Holy Spirit to GO... to travel the roads and tell of what she *had seen and heard.* She needed the journeys to launch her testimony and establish her conquest: a new tabernacle, more souls who loved and praised their God.

That a woman, one who, moreover, was an enclosed nun, and, to crown it all, who presented herself as a champion of reform, should spend most of her time

"This is how the Saint travelled": reconstruction her arrival at Villanueva de la Jara.

on the road was something which her contemporaries found very hard to take; probably the single most disconcerting thing about her.

Her superiors took her to task for it, as did two successive Nuncios — Ormaneto and Sega. The former was her friend and did it gently — through Fr. Gracián; the latter, influenced by Calced opposition, was quite harsh about it. His is the famous description of her as "a restless gadabout of a woman."

Even her biographers were not too happy about this aspect of her life. Ribera, for example, devotes a whole chapter of his biography to explaining why she had to do it. Simple people, too, did not understand. One day Teresa, to make conversation with one of

the muleteers, told him she was travelling to earn her reward in Heaven. Somewhat taken aback, he replied that he could get to Heaven from home and didn't need such complications.

Yet, one of the most characteristic features of this "gadabout" was that she took her lifestyle with her when she travelled. Here is Gracián's account of what it was like to travel with her:

"I want to describe now how she travelled; I accompanied her quite a lot and to many places.

Usually, three of us religious and some laymen accompanied her. Before we arrived at an inn, she would send one of us ahead to order food and reserve rooms. One of the latter had always to be sufficiently

large to allow all the nuns to stay together. Everything they would need had to be put in that room, so that they wouldn't have to ask for anything and the maids would have no reason to go in there...

They always lowered their veils when they left the wagon, and the first thing we always did, if it was the right time for it, was to attend Mass, at which the Saint would receive Holy Communion.

Once in their room, she closed the door and appointed a door-keeper, just as if she were in a monastery. Very often she was ill, and since the sisters couldn't go out to the kitchen one of us did the cooking. This amused her greatly, though the sisters would have been happier if they could do more for her....

Sometimes the rooms had no doors. Then she would place us outside to ensure that no one could come in. In some inns the nuns were not able to have a room to themselves. We would then bring in some blankets and hang them to form a screen so that the nuns would always have privacy.

That way, the nuns could ring their little bell for periods of silence, personal prayer, or the Divine Service, as they did in the wagon, just as if they were in their monastery.

The Mother's solicitude for the needs of those who travelled with her was remarkable. One would think she thought of nothing else... Sometimes she spoke so charmingly to those who accompanied us on foot that they forgot their weariness.

At times we travelled on mule-back, riding along and chatting about Godly things; she rode as well and as steadily as if she were in a carriage. Once, her mule took fright and bolted. She brought it under control herself, with no screams or other expression of female panic.''

And so the time passed — reminiscing, writing and praying — until at last that happy day came when she was permitted to resume her travels once more. Four years have passed and she is now ''a little old woman,'' to use her own expression. Besides, she has lost the use of her left arm ever since the devil threw her down the stairs in Avila. But she still has enough energy and drive to take to the roads once more, though from now on she would always be accompanied by her faithful nurse and secretary, Sister, now Blessed, Anne of St. Bartholomew.

She began by visiting most of her monasteries — Medina, Valladolid, Alba de Tormes, Salamanca, Avila, and even as far as Malagón. Needless to say, she was received with open arms and great joy everywhere, after an absence which had been as painful as it was long.

Petitions were pouring in from all sides for her to come and found — calls from Zamora, Madrid, Valencia, Lisbon, etc. But the Lord did not direct her to these great places; He pointed to the little village of Villanueva de la Jara, a haven of peace set in the fertile plains of the province of Cuenca.

The background to this choice is closely connected with the famous penitent, Catalina de Cardona, who lived in a cave only four leagues from Villanueva. Her incredibly ascetic life was bound to have some influence on the people of the surrounding district. Thus it was that some young ladies of the village were fired with her enthusiasm and shut themselves away in a house by St. Anne's hermitage. It was really a house of *beatas,* but they were determined to make it an austere monastery. They read the works of St. Peter of Alcántara and Fray Luis de Granada for guidance, observed enclosure, and supported themselves by the work of their hands.

The fact that Catalina's spiritual directors were the Discalced Carmelite Fathers of nearby La Roda, and that these were well-known in Villanueva de la Jara for their preaching, made the Carmelite Order a fairly obvious choice when the above-mentioned young ladies looked about for an Order to which they could attach themselves.

This is how Teresa describes the events leading up to her decision to found there:

"When I was in Toledo in 1576 after founding the

Exterior of the Carmelite convent, Villanueva de la Jara.

Seville monastery, a cleric from Villanueva de la Jara brought me a letter from the local council desiring to negotiate with me about receiving nine women who were living together in a hermitage into one of my communities."

Her first reaction was to turn the proposition down flat: Villanueva was too far away the other foundations, resources seemed insufficient, people accustomed to a particular life style would have difficulty adapting themselves to the Carmelite rule, they hadn't got a house of their own, and Teresa had not seen them. As she said herself, "I had been told that they were very good, but since I hadn't seen them myself I didn't know if they were suitable for what we

expect of people in our monasteries. So I decided to drop the idea entirely" (F.28,9)

Nevertheless, as was her custom, she postponed a final decision until she had consulted some learned man, her confessor, and God on the subject.

Meanwhile, during the ensuing time of persecution, the request was repeatedly renewed with ever-increasing urgency. The prior of the nearby community of La Roda joined in the chorus, as did her old friend Fr. Antonio de Jesús, now also a member of that community.

As nearly always happened, the final push came from the Lord himself: "One day just after Holy Communion I was raising up this matter before the Lord, as I had often done before... and His Majesty took me severely to task. He asked me what kind of treasures I had needed to accomplish what had been done up to then, and told me to have no doubts about accepting this house. It would render Him great service and benefit souls, He said" (F.28,15).

Mother Teresa had been in Malagón about ten weeks when this happened. She was quite ill, but set out nevertheless in the company of the two La Roda friars already mentioned. They set out on their twenty-eight league journey on 13 February 1580.

Their passage through the intervening villages was like a triumphal march. The village folk knew the friars and had often heard them extol her virtues. Now, they turned out *en masse* to greet her. They vied with one another in hospitality, they entertained her and even brought the cattle out for her to bless. The friars of La Roda came in procession to greet her and persuaded her to stay a few days with them. No wonder her health showed a marked improvement! On 21 February, the first Sunday in Lent, they reached their destination.

"The whole municipality and several other people, including Doctor Ervías (parish priest) came out to greet us. We went first to the village church, which was

Well in the convent courtyard. It goes back to the Saint's time.

Garden and convent, Villanueva de la Jara.

quite a distance from that of St. Anne. Such was the joy of the whole village that I was greatly comforted to see them receive the Order of Our Blessed Lady in that way. We could hear the bells pealing long before we reached it. When we entered the church they intoned the *Te Deum...* After that they placed the Blessed Sacrament and a statue of Our Lady on two portable platforms, and we set out in solemn procession with crosses and banners... As there was quite a distance to go, they had set up altars at various points along the way, and stopped from time to time to recite something about our Order. We found it very devotional... and were moved at seeing so much attention paid to seven poor Discalced nuns for God's sake'' (F.28,37).

The new foundation, then, was inaugurated on the day of their arrival; it was dedicated to St. Anne.

Mother Teresa showed so much consideration and affection for these *beatas* that they never forgot it, and the memory of her beneficial influence during the month she stayed there lingered among the villagers as well. One day someone came during recreation time asking to see Mother Teresa. When the nuns expressed some displeasure at her leaving them, she said: ''My recreation is to comfort the afflicted.'' The afflicted in this case was a poor woman whose children were all born dead. Mother Teresa gave instructions that her belt be given to the woman. From then on many women found a remedy for maternity-related problems through St. Teresa's belt.

Visiting this old monastery today one can still see parts of the original buildings, though their function has changed. The parlours are *the original hermitage;* Teresa divided it into a chapel and choir. The present sacristy and revolving window area is where *the nuns' living quarters* once were. The old *well and winch,* where a mason once accidentally hurt Mother Teresa, are still there. And they treasure a statue of the Child Jesus which Teresa presented to them as a gift.

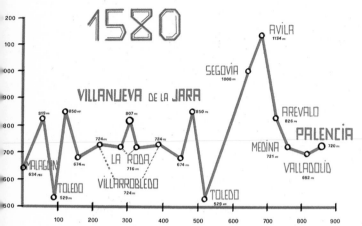

1580

AVILA 1134 m		
SEGOVIA 1000 m		
VILLANUEVA DE LA JARA		
AREVALO 826 m		
PALENCIA		
819 m · 850 MP · 807 m · 850 m · MEDINA 721 m · 720 m		
724 m · LA RODA 716 m · 724 m · VALLADOLID 692 m		
MALAGON 634 m · 674 m · 674 m		
TOLEDO 529 m · VILLARROBLEDO 724 m · TOLEDO 529 m		

Journey to Palencia.

Foundation of the Carmelite convent in Palencia from the "Book of the Foundations": "JHS deals with the foundation of St. Joseph of Our Lady of the Way in Palencia, in the year MDLXXX, on the feast of King David."

PALENCIA

St. Teresa's route on the way to Palencia 1580-1581

— *summer-autumn 1580: the Saint suffered a long illness, having succumbed to the condition known as the "universal cold." She became "aged" and weak. As soon as she recovered, she embarked on the next foundation.*

— *December 28th: Teresa set out from Valladolid for Palencia.*

— *December 29th: she installed the new carmel at Palencia; but continued looking for a suitable house.*

— *February 1581: preparations for the decisive "separation Chapter" came to a head at Alcalá. Mother Teresa and her nuns sent briefs.*

— *early March: inauguration of the Chapter at Alcalá. The Saint followed it attently from Palencia.*

— *March 4th: Fr. Gracián was elected the Discalceds' Provincial.*

— *April 9th: Gracián granted Teresa a licence to found in Burgos; but this foundation was to be delayed.*

— *May 26th: the community moved definitively to its new monastery.*

— *May 29th 1581: the Saint left Palencia, heading for Soria.*

A Carmelite nun of the Order of Carmel.

— *Mother Teresa belonged to the religious family officially known as "the Brothers of Our Lady of Mount Carmel," founded in the early 13th century at Mount Carmel, Israel, from whence the Order soon had to emigrate to Europe.*

— *Mother Teresa became a Carmelite at the convent of the Incarnation in Avila (founded in 1479). She lived there for 27 years as a nun (1535-1562); and three years as prioress (1571-1574).*

— *She founded a new branch of Carmelites in 1562 and in 1581 saw it raised to the status of Province; but it was not until after the Saint's death that it became a canonically autonomous religious family.*

— *The Carmelites who assisted the Saint in her labour of founding monasteries were: the Prior General of the Order, Juan Bautista Rubeo, who withdrew his support around 1575; the Provincial for Castile, Angel de Salazar, who later gave evidence at the proceedings for the Saint's beatification; Fr. John of the Cross, a pioneer member of the group of Teresian monks; and Fr. Jerónimo Diego Gracián, who was the group's first provincial and the most deeply identified with the person and philosophy of the Foundress.*

View of the convent in Palencia during the last century: drawing by Hye Hoys (1866-1867).

PALENCIA
ST. JOSEPH OF OUR LADY OF THE STREET
29.12.1580

Back in Toledo once more after her triumphal visit to Villanueva de la Jara, Teresa met Fr. Gracián and both of them sat down to plan the realisation of one of Teresa's most cherished ambitions — to found in Madrid.

With that haste which characterises the servants of God, who think they must do a lot because there is so much to do and who think it must be done quickly for life is so short, they both set to work. Teresa assured him that a house and money would be forthcoming, and that she had already trained her cousin Inés de Jesús to be prioress. All that was lacking was the permission of the archbishop of Toledo. Whatever the obstacles involved, they would obtain an audience with this august personage, Cardinal Quiroga.

All went smoothly. The Cardinal Primate of Spain and its colonies, who was also the Grand Inquisitor, received them on the feast of Corpus Christi. He

Santo Cristo del Otero, on the outskirts of Palencia.

Statue of Our Lady of the Way.

couldn't have been nicer to them and they left his presence full of enthusiasm.

According to Gracián, the cardinal was delighted to meet Mother Teresa, as he had been wishing to do so for some time. He assured her that she could count on him as a chaplain at her orders. He recalled the sad fact of her *Life* being sent to the Inquisition. They had carefully examined it, he said, and decided that it contained safe and profitable teaching; in fact, he had read it himself from cover to cover. The required permission was granted very readily and the cardinal asked Mother Teresa to pray for him.

But — God's ways again! as Teresa would have said. In spite of having all they needed, Teresa would not live to see a Carmelite monastery in Madrid.

She now went on to Segovia, where she learned of the death of her favourite brother, Lorenzo; a painful loss tempered by the hope of her faith. This meant that she now had to look after the immediate problems of his three orphan children. The influenza epidemic of that year carried off several of her closest friends as well.

After visiting Avila and Medina, Teresa herself became gravely ill in Valladolid. She had been sent there at the request of Don Alvaro de Mendoza, bishop of Palencia, the man who as bishop of Avila had helped her start the reform and had been a great friend ever since. "Our Lord laid it on his heart that a monastery of our Order should be founded there too. When I reached Valladolid, I fell so gravely ill that they thought I would die" (F.29,1).

Not that another illness was anything new to Mother

Teresa; to a greater or lesser degree she was always ill. Her spirit dwelt in heavenly places while her body slowly crumbled. What we have here is one more instance of physical incapacity putting a brake on her reforming drive. This time it was more serious, however, and it is worth our while to pause a moment and think about it.

"Without illnesses there is no Teresa of Jesus," writes Donázar. Another author, Azorín, also comments on illness in her life: "Perhaps the most attractive characteristic of her life's work is provided by her illnesses. After all, the Teresian Reform is really an intensely dramatic struggle, a heroic work against everything and everybody, a fight carried on without health or money. In those difficult moments when all seemed lost, there is St. Teresa lying on her sickbed behind the parlour grille, forcing herself to speak, obliged to negotiate with people, striving to convince, trying to go on...."

Yes, Mother Teresa knew all about moral and physical weakness. And when she speaks of the latter she distinguishes very clearly between real weakness and those brought on by psychical conditions, such as melancholy or being too fond of ourselves.

It was probably this constant struggle with the weakness of her own body that prompted her to leave such a wealth of descriptions of various illnesses and complaints throughout her writings, and so many words of advice on the care of the body. In fact, she mentions so many specific cures that there is quite an amount of literature on her medical knowledge. Unfortunately, that too is a subject we cannot enlarge upon here.

Let's get back, then, to the Saint's bedside. She recovered slowly, but this time it took a lot out of her. Fr. Gracián noticed the change — tired, and looking her age for the first time. "I was so weak," she says, "that I even lost that confidence which God always gave me when I was starting a new monastery. Everything looked impossible to me" (F.29,3).

But they kept at her to make the Palencia foundation: she owed it to bishop Mendoza, they said; "they" being the prioress of Valladolid and her one-time confessors Frs. Ripalda and Báñez. Their importunings, even their efforts to encourage her, were of no avail. And then one day all that changed: "One day, after Communion, when I was full of doubts and undecided about either of the foundations (by this time Burgos was being spoken of as well), I beseeched Our Lord to give me light so that I would do His will. That desire did not leave me notwithstanding all my lassitude. The Lord said reproachfully: 'What are you afraid of? When have I let you down? I am now the same as I have always been, so be sure to make both foundations.' O great God, how different are your words to those spoken by men!" (F.29,6).

Suddenly, she was her old self again and lost no time in getting things moving. In his little autobiographical book *Peregrinación de Anastasio,* Fr. Gracián takes up the story: "She sent me to take a look at the place and report on the lie of the land, for she was a woman who liked to be well-informed about everything before undertaking a foundation. I went to Palencia and was somewhat discouraged by the priests of the cathedral there: it was a poor town, they said, and the nuns would not be able to support themselves. I was returning with my mind made up not to make that foundation, when I met Suero de Vega... an impor-

Palencia Cathedral.

encountered a fog so dense that at times they couldn't even see one another.

Six nuns accompanied Mother Teresa, as well as the Valladolid chaplain and an admirer called D. Agustín de Vitoria. It was just as well that the journey was short, for what with the rigours of the winter and the freezing fog they were petrified by the time they reached Palencia. Just as well, too, that Teresa had sent word of their arrival and asked Canon Reinoso to have everything ready for them. The kindly priest had done exactly as he was told; food, light, beds were all ready.

The house was in the populous La Puebla part of town and had a fine doorway with a magnificent arch above it set in a pretty stone façade.

Next day, at that time the feast of King David, of whom Teresa was an ardent admirer, the first Mass was celebrated and the community installed.

The whole city reacted to this new Carmel with considerable enthusiasm. Bishop Mendoza was the first to visit the nuns; he enquired after their welfare and gave instructions for a quantity of bread to be delivered to them daily. The city *Corregidor,* who had only reluctantly consented to their coming in the first place, joined in the general acclaim with a phrase that has become famous: "Mother Teresa must have in her bosom some authorization from the Royal Council of God, which makes us do whatever she wants whether we like it or not."

Later, with the help of Canons Reinoso and Salinas, Teresa bought a chapel dedicated to Our Lady of the Street, and the adjoining houses. The community moved there during the octave of Corpus Christi, 1581. They stayed only ten years there, however, for accommodation was cramped and anyway Canon Reinoso offered them his own house. Unfortunately, they had spent all they had on alterations and, helped by the city's own circumstances, experienced great poverty. God sent them relief in the form of a very rich novice, Doña Luisa de Aragón, whose fortune solved all these financial difficulties. At a still later date, the community moved again; this time to the outskirts of town on the Burgos side, and that is where they are today.

Her settling in the hermitage where there was a shrine

tant and very spiritual man... He gave me great encouragement and afterwards helped the monastery generously."

Having received Gracián's favourable report, and a letter from Canon Reinoso placing himself entirely at her disposal, Teresa set a date for the foundation: they would leave on 28 December and inaugurate the new monastery the following day, it being only 50 kilometres to Palencia.

They set out as planned, but as their route followed the courses of the Pisuerga and Carrión Rivers they

Rueca de Santa Teresa de Jesús

Distaff used by the Saint.

to Our Lady of the Street reminds us that this decision fitted in perfectly with another of Teresa's chief ideas — that she lived in the Blessed Virgin's house. She always thought of her Order and each Carmel in it as being Our Lady's family.

This devotion went back to her childhood, in particular to the death of her mother when Teresa was only thirteen. Her reaction to that death was to run to the picture of Our Lady of Charity and tearfully ask Our Lady to be her mother. "Though I was rather naïve, I think my prayer was heard, because I was conscious of finding this sovereign Virgin as soon as I commended myself to her" (L.1,7).

As she left the Incarnation for St. Joseph's, she 'discalced' herself, that is took her shoes off, before Our Lady's shrine in the crypt of San Vicente.

She handed her the keys of the Incarnation and named her Prioress, as we've seen.

She felt her near in many of the visions with which Our Lord blessed her.

Her joy in Villanueva de la Jara was at seeing so many people honour "Our Lady's habit."

Her last foundation would be dedicated to Mary's family, and, of course, wherever Jesus was honoured

with a statue or picture in one of her convents there was bound to be one of Our Lady nearby.

Nor was Teresa's knowledge of Mary purely external. Mary was part of her "interior life" and perceived in the context of her mystical experiences. The mysteries of her co-redemption and glorification had special significance for her, and left their mark on her teaching.

Some of all this, indeed maybe more than this, must have passed through Teresa's mind as she took possession of the little hermitage of Our Lady of the Street in Palencia. A great favour she received while staying there also had something to do with her love for Mary. It was here she received the *Brief separating Discalced from Calced,* a document by which the Pope, claiming to have been enlightened by the Blessed Virgin, finally made peace between the two branches of the Carmelite Order.

Relics of Teresa's passage through Palencia are: an *ablution bowl* (for the priest to wash his fingers after Communion), a *coif,* two *chairs,* a *tambourine and castanets,* the above-mentioned *Brief,* which she ordered to be incorporated in the community minute book, and numerous other objects.

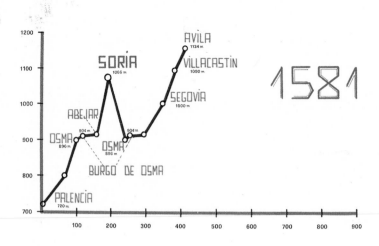

Journey to Soria, and return to Avila.

SORIA

St. Teresa's route
from Palencia to Soria
1581

— May 29th 1581: the Saint and her nuns set out from Palencia for Soria.
— June 2nd: she arrived in Soria, where Bishop Alonso Velázquez was waiting for her.
— June 3rd: the Soria convent was founded.
— August 16th: Teresa began the return journey from Soria to Avila.
— August 23rd: she arrived in Avila.
— September 4th-5th: Mother Teresa spent the night at Villacastín, weary and "well tired of walking."
— September 6th: she arrived at St. Joseph's in Avila, where she was elected prioress on the 10th.
— November 28th: Fr. John of the Cross reached Avila, anxious to take the Saint to the Granada foundation. He did not succeed, for she was already preparing to found in Burgos.
— November 29th: St. John of the Cross left Avila for Granada, without Mother Teresa.

Account the foundation in the "Book of the Foundations": "Beginning of the foundation of the convent of the Holy Trinity in the city of Soria. It was founded in the year MDLXXXI. The first Mass was celebrated on the feast of our Father St. Elisha."

The gadabout's interior.
— In 1581 Teresa wrote her last introspective piece, like a great balcony giving onto the landscape of the soul itself: Relation IV, addressed to Don Alonso Velázquez, Bishop of Osma and Soria.
— Since 1560, a powerful inner call had compelled her to follow a programme of regular pauses to study her own inner state. Her success is recorded in a series of brief, intimate texts called the Relations. 67 have survived to our day: a collection of real jewels.
— The last glimpse was unsurpassable: absolute peace on the horizon of the soul, awaiting arrival on the final shore.

Exterior of the Carmelite convent in Soria: drawing by Hye Hoys (1866-1867).

SORIA
MONASTERY OF THE BLESSED TRINITY
14.6.1581.

It is said that as Teresa travelled towards Soria she said: ''Daughters, when we get to Soria, which is the end of the world, there must be no turning back; you must go on working for God.'' The phrase ''Forward by all means, but nobody must turn back'' became an insistent refrain.

Teresa knew too much about faraway places to think the world ended at Soria. What she was referring to surely was that the end of the road was in sight for herself. And she wanted to make it clear that they must not stop when she was gone; ''always forward'' must still be their motto.

Teresa really intended going on to Burgos once the necessary alterations had been made to the hermitage of Our Lady of the Street in Palencia. Writing to

Overall view of Soria.

Canon Reinoso she even mentioned likely sites for such a foundation. But, as often before, "God's ways" and Teresa's plans did not always coincide.

God had a way of putting people in her path to help her, people to whom she had reason to be grateful. One of these now asked her to bring her nuns to Soria. He was Don Alonso Velázquez, a learned and holy canon who had helped her greatly with encouragement and advice in the difficult days at Toledo. He was now bishop of Osma-Soria and engaged in the reform of religious life in his diocese. If she would only come to Soria, he had a noble lady who would give all the help they needed. Just let him know, and he would send for her, he said.

Teresa couldn't refuse a friend like Dr. Velázquez. It would be nice sharing with him again about Godly things, and she would add another decade to her rosary of carmels.

So the usual foundation machine was set in motion: consultation, recruitment, journey.

The prioress chosen for the new monastery was
Catalina de Cristo from the Medina Carmel. Fr.
Gracián was unimpressed, to say the least; she was
barely literate. "Never mind," said Teresa, "she loves
God a great deal, is very holy, deeply spiritual, and
she doesn't need any more than that to govern pro-
perly." Another nun from Medina, two each from
Salamanca, Segovia, and Palencia, and Mother
Teresa was ready. She also asked Frs. Nicholas Doria
and Elisco de la Madre de Dios along.

The journey proved a welcome change in Teresa's
state of health. Doña Beatriz de Beaumont — who
was financing the foundation — sent a carriage to
fetch them and her chaplain to wait upon their needs.
The bishop sent a servant and a policeman to make
sure everything was in readiness at the inns along the
way. Nor was the bishop of Palencia going to be out-
done in generosity; he instructed the cathedral bursar
to see the party had all they needed for the journey.
The weather obliged, the company was pleasant, the
country was flat. In fact, the only cloud on the proceedings was the absence of Fr. Gracián.

Looking back on this journey in a letter, Teresa recalled that "Though journeys generally tired me out,
that from Palencia to Soria was like an outing. It was
a smooth journey and much of it close to rivers,
which I loved." There were no fewer than six rivers in
that area, and, with her love of water, they must have
lightened her heart considerably.

After stopping the first night at Encinas de Esgueva,
the following day they reached Aranda and so

Façade of the Carmelite convent, Soria.

Ruins of San Juan de Duero.

Santo Domingo church.

crossed into the diocese of Osma. The policeman was on home ground now and threw his weight about a bit. Teresa was highly amused at his antics, yet grateful for his ability to obtain the best treatment for them.

Apparently not everyone was amused at the sight of a policeman escorting the party. In one place they misread the situation and berated him, thinking he was taking them to the Inquisition!

Another little anecdote about this journey concerns the faith of the country folk in Teresa's powers of intercession with God. They asked her to obtain much-needed rain for their crops. Teresa, moved by their distress, began to recite the Litany to the Saints with her companions. It rained immediately.

On May 30th they stayed overnight at the guesthouse of the great Premonstratensian monastery of Our Lady of the Vine. Next day they reached the little walled town of Burgo de Osma. The bishop resided there, but had gone ahead to await their arrival in Soria. The population — some 300 — stayed indoors; apparently just then there was a plague scare and nobody was taking any chances.

One more night on the road, and at last Soria lay before them, its extensive and imposing walls clearly visible from afar. There had been a time when these walls held a population of seven or eight thousand; now there were fewer, but it still had some fine houses.

The view from the Duero.

Interior of the Carmelite convent.

The party reached Soria about 5 p.m. and were escorted by a mounted guard of honour amid cheering crowds.

"The lady who was our foundress was waiting at the door of her house, which was where the monastery was going to be. We were relieved to be inside, for there was a great crowd around us... The lady had seen fully to our every need" (F.30,8).

Doña Beatriz de Beaumont, or Beaumonte as she is sometimes referred to in Spanish, was descended from the kings of Navarre and was a daughter of the captain general of the Imperial Guard. According to Teresa, she was kindly, generous, penitent and a great servant of God. Widowed, and having no children, she spent her whole fortune on works of piety and on her relatives. Two years after the Soria carmel was founded, she helped generously with that of Pamplona. At sixty she entered that monastery herself and lived there a further seventeen years.

With a woman like that Teresa had no difficulties over contractual details. In fact, she reminded her sisters on numerous occasions to treat her with great love.

To return to our story, it only remains to note that the official opening took place on 14 June 1581, Feast of St. Eliseus. The bishop himself celebrated the inaugural Mass, and the monastery was dedicated to the Blessed Trinity.

The bishop also donated a church next door and had a covered passage built to connect it with the

monastery. This and other works were completed by Ausgust 5th, Feast of the Transfiguration, an event which was also celebrated with due solemnity.

In speaking of the reasons why Teresa liked the idea of going to Soria we mentioned that she looked forward to being able to discuss spiritual matters with Dr. Velázquez. She was now able to do so with all the freedom and devotion she enjoyed in his presence, and which she speaks of at length in the chapter dealing with this foundation.

She told him of the "uninterrupted intellectual vision" of the Trinity and the Humanity of Christ she now experienced. How it was compatible with a busy life. Of the tremendous peace it brought. Of the full awareness it gave of God's presence in her soul.

We don't know what the holy bishop had to say to all that. What emerges from her side of the conversation is the feeling that this exceptional woman had arrived at where the way of prayer was meant to lead. She had reached her destination.

Yet there had been a time in her life when Teresa, destined to be called "Mother of Spiritual People" and to be the first woman to be declared a Doctor of the Church, was a failure in prayer. But she picked herself up again, and discovered true Christian prayer through experience rather than books. Through her determination to be stopped by nothing, whatever it might cost, she reached the spiritual fulfilment in which we now see her.

What really put her on the road was the discovery that prayer was communication between friends, frequent conversation with one who we know loves us. It is the ability to relate on a personal level with the transcendental God, to treat Him as a friend who is near enough to bring him our worries and problems, even our very lives.

Where prayer was concerned, Teresa was a disciple before she became a teacher. Her long and deep experience of it was worth a thousand treatises. She was convinced that prayer, like so many other things, was best learned by getting down and doing it.
When she teaches, therefore, she speaks from experience. She had encountered the difficulties, knew

Façade of the church.

Interior courtyard in the convent of Soria.

Statue of St. Teresa (Carmelite convent, Soria).

Rooms formerly used as workshops (Soria convent).

how humility and self-denial helped, was familiar with the stages one went through, knew that prayer was the only door to the interior castle at the centre of which God dwells, and that true prayer transformed one's life and developed with it. After all, prayer and living are the measure of one another.

Today we live in a world in which we have succeeded in establishing contact with the stars, in which the widest possible communication has become a felt need and given a great impetus to the study of languages and symbols. And yet we are practically illiterate when it comes to the one language we really need to know. Only when we are convinced that to really communicate with God, to discover the inner world of our spirit, and to benefit our fellow-man, prayer is necessary, will we try and learn how to do it. If we take Mother Teresa as our tutor it will be only a matter of learning our mother tongue.

When her presence was no longer needed at Soria, Teresa returned to Avila via Segovia. She had few companions and found the return journey as hard and painful as the outward trip had been enjoyable.

The monastery she left behind has changed but little since. Among its mementoes of those bygone days it treasures *The Virgin of the Five Towns,* a present to Teresa from Dr. Velázquez; the old safe, called the ark of the three keys, and a few other objects dating back to the time of its foundation.

The 'Virgin of the Five Towns.'

Gold doubloon, a present of the Saint's to Diego de Yepes, later her biographer.

Church of St. Stephen in Gormaz.

An old portrait of the Saint (in the Carmelite convent).

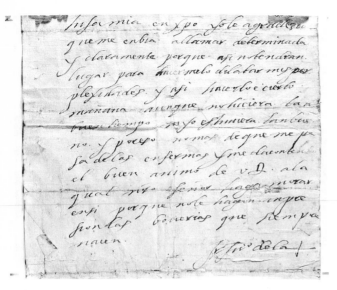

Autograph of St. John of the Cross.

Granada on the map of the Peninsula.

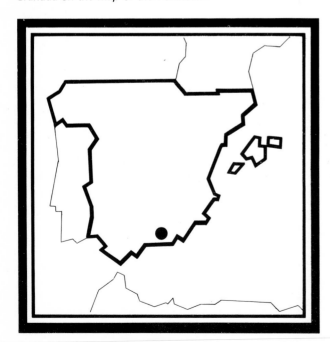

GRANADA

Fr. John of the Cross's route
from Avila to Granada

— *June 28th 1581: St. John of the Cross was in Caravaca (Murcia).*
In the following months he visited several different cities in Andalusia.
— *mid-November 1581: Fr. John of the Cross travelled to Avila. He outlined to the Saint the plan to found a convent in Granada; but did not succeed in having the Foundress leave with him.*
— *November 28th 1581: the two Saints' last conversation. Fr. John set out for Andalusia: he would not meet Mother Teresa again.*
— *first fortnight of December: he arrived at Beas, accompanied by two future foundresses of the Granada carmel.*
— *January: the three travelled from Beas to Granada.*
— *January 19th: they arrived in Granada.*
— *January 20th: the convent was founded, albeit only provisionally.*
— *May 30th: St. Teresa wrote a long letter from Burgos containing instructions for the prioress at Granada, Anne of Jesus.*

A pair of teachers, Teresa de Jesús and John of the Cross.
— *The peculiarity of their relationship was that they were both teacher and disciple, reciprocally.*
— *When the two met at Medina (1567), Teresa was almost 52 years old, Fr. John only 25. She had already determined the vocation of her life and religion: a Carmelite and a foundress. He was still searching, and hesitated between the Carthusian order and the Carmel. Mother Teresa recruited him and trained him.*
— *Four years later (1571-72) she, as prioress of the Incarnation, confided the spiritual teaching at the convent (where there many nuns) to Fr. John of the Cross; and herself became his disciple. She was never to repudiate this teaching; she confirmed his authority when Fr. John began to exercise as a spiritual master in the Andalusian carmels — Beas, Granada, Caravaca and Seville.*
— *After Mother Teresa's death, Fr. John of the Cross was one of the first teologians to recognise and recommend her spiritual theachings. He proclaimed this explicitly in his Spiritual Canticle (verse 13, 7), referring to her books and arguing that they should be published as soon as possible.*

Exterior of the Carmelite convent, Granada: drawing by Hye Hoys (1866-1867).

GRANADA
MONASTERY OF ST. JOSEPH
20.1.1582.

The foundation of Granada Carmel has the distinction of being the only one in Teresa's lifetime which she

was neither present at nor described in her *Foundations.* She had two eminent people to take her place, however: John of the Cross and Anne of Jesus (Lobera).

Teresa had been back in Avila about ten weeks, ironing out some problems there, when John of the Cross arrived with a petition to found in Granada. Some devout people in the city had promised to make available enough money to the Vicar Provincial of Andalusia to cover all expenses.

This time Teresa felt she should go ahead with the

Overall view of the Alhambra.

plans which were already made for Burgos; hence her delegation of the Granada project to the two persons mentioned above.

As usual their best-laid plans went awry. The promised help did not materialise and the bishop refused permission. Undaunted, the party proceeded to Granada, only to find that the man who had agreed to rent them a house changed his mind when he found out that it was to be a convent. If a holy widow called Doña Ana de Peñalosa, to whom John of the Cross was spiritual director, had not taken them into her house, they could well have found themselves on the street.

Anne of Jesus decided to go and see the bishop again. By one of those neat accidents of Providence he happened to be frightened out of his wits the day she called. A thunderbolt had narrowly missed his bedroom the night before. He took the hint, so to speak, and promptly gave his permission.

The foundation was inaugurated in Doña Ana's house on 20 January 1582, and dedicated to St. Joseph. It was another six months before the nuns were able to rent a house of their own. But then several rich young ladies took the habit and the following year they were able to buy the Duke of Sesa's palace.

Among the relics preserved there today are some *fragments of St. Teresa's flesh,* her *renunciation of the Mitigated Rule,* her *cross* and *walking stick,* and the *cell* where she appeared to Anne of Jesus just after her death and restored her to health.

Overall view of Los Mártires (Granada).

Central cloister of the Carmelite convent.

The Saint's staff (Granada).

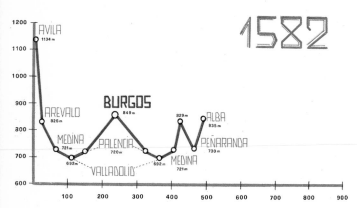

Last journeys: to Burgos and Alba.

St. Teresa's route
Burgos, the last task
1582

— Winter. January 2nd 1582: the Saint left Avila, accompanied by Father Gracián.
— January 4th: they arrived at Medina and paused briefly.
— January 9th: they arrived in Valladolid and rested for four days.
— January 14th: they set out for Palencia. They stopped at length there, for more than a week.
— January 24th: St. Teresa and Father Gracián left Palencia in the direction of Burgos.
— January 26th, at nightfall: they arrived in Burgos.
— January 23rd: the Saint and her nuns set up house in the Hospital of the Immaculate Conception.
— March 12th: purchase of the Mansino house.
— March 18th: Mother Teresa moved to the new house.
— April 14th: Catalina de Tolosa donated the Burgos convent by deed.
— April 18th-19th: the Archbishop granted permission and the new carmel was founded.
— May 7th: Gracián took his leave of St. Teresa. They were never to meet again.
— May 23rd: the Arlanzón overflowed its banks and flooded the new convent.
— July 27th: the Saint left Burgos.
— end of July: at Palencia.
— August 20th: she arrived in Valladolid.
— September 15th: she set out from Valladolid for Medina, arriving on the 16th.
— September 19th: Teresa left Medina. By order of Father Antonio she did not continue the journey to Avila, but made for Alba.
— September 20th, at nightfall: she arrived at Alba de Tormes. Exhausted, she went to bed.
— October 4th, about 9 pm: St. Teresa died at Alba.

Teresian foundations during the life of the Saint:

Convents:
Avila, Medina, Malagón, Valladolid, Toledo, Pastrana, Salamanca, Alba, Segovia, Beas, Seville, Caravaca, Villanueva de la Jara, Palencia, Soria, Granada, Burgos. Altogether, 17 carmels.

Monasteries for monks:
Duruelo-Mancera, Pastrana, Alcalá de Henares, Altomira, La Roda, Granada, La Peñuela, Seville, El Calvario, Almodóvar del Campo, Valladolid, Salamanca, Lisbon. Altogether, 13 monasteries.

Autograph account of the foundation of the Carmelite convent in Burgos, from the "Book of the Foundations": "In this chapter we begin to describe the foundation of the glorious St. Joseph of St. Anne in the city of Burgos. The first Mass was said on 19th April, octave of Easter, in the year MDLXXXII."

Exterior of the Carmelite convent in Burgos: drawing by Hye Hoys (1866-1867).

BURGOS
MONASTERY OF ST. JOSEPH AND ST. ANNE
19.4.1582

We now reach the 31st and last chapter of the *Foundations,* Teresa's lengthy account of her last adventure, written about the end of June 1582, just a few months before her death. Nowhere do we find the slightest hint of a tired pen. Quite the contrary in fact; it is a lively tale full of conflict and drama. Three stages stand out: the planning of the undertaking, the apparently inextricable knot of complications, and the happy ending.

In this account Teresa appears for the last time. Without meaning to, she describes herself: her body is extremely frail, suffering from the cold, but her spirit is still on fire and driving it on. She is vigorous and firm. Even when events throw Fr. Gracián out of sorts, no difficulty gets her down.

Part of the city of Burgos.

Nor does she let the initiative slip from her grasp. It is she who founds. She may have to direct operations from her bed, hardly able to speak with a sore throat, but she does the directing. And that means attending to a lot more than immediate arrangements. She maintains continual contacts with the friends and supporters of this venture. She writes to the bishop of Palencia urging him to intervene. The day she receives confirmation that a house has been bought, she writes to Lisbon, where the King, the nuncio and the Duke of Alba are, to obtain permission to sing Mass in the house; this is something she is finding extremely difficult to extract from the archbishop of Burgos.

When all the work is done, more writing awaits her: the final pages of the *Foundations*. These pages are packed with the most extraordinary handwriting. Not an erasion, no sign of hesitancy; just a slight tremble in the hand, perhaps, but showing all the vigour of youth in those slightly upward slanting lines. The con-

tent, too, shows complete clarity of mind. Fr. Gracián himself couldn't have described the foundation better.

What characterises her account of the Burgos foundation most of all, however, is the interweaving of the divine and human elements. Here God is at once the leading character and a spectator. His words are passed on to us quite unselfconsciously: sober words, spoken at the right moment, without any connotations of their being extraordinary. His presence is taken for granted and his words recorded as if His speaking was the most natural thing in the world.

So we reach the beginning of the end. ''For more than six years, some very senior men in the Society of Jesus, learned and spiritual men, had been telling me that Our Lord would be well pleased to have a house of our Order in Burgos. Their arguments in its favour made me too desire this. But the trials which the Order was enduring and other foundations gave me no opportunity of doing so'' (F.31,1). So little opportunity did she have, in fact, that she very nearly didn't get to either of her most cherished goals: Burgos and Madrid.

If Madrid proved attractive because it was convenient to the Court, where so much business had to be done, Burgos had the attraction of being a great and famous city. It boasted of a high quota of nobility and had the name of being very Christian, with an unusually high number of charitable institutions.

In Teresa's day Burgos had lost much of its ancient splendour, but it was still the most important city in Old Castile. It had a population of about 8,000, among them some of very noble lineage and not a few wealthy merchants.

To quote a description dating from the days of El Cid, ''It was a large city divided in two by a river, each part having its own walls. Strong and wealthy, it had large commercial enterprises, markets, wheat exchanges, and warehouses.'' In the 16th century it still had the two walls, and its inhabitants had the name of being the most refined, honourable and hospitable people in the whole of Spain.

Monastery of Las Huelgas (Burgos).

Crucifix in Burgos Cathedral.

The spiritual needs of its population were catered for by thirteen parishes, as well as famous abbeys, a university and numerous houses of friars.

St. Teresa experienced great difficulty in getting a foothold in Burgos, as we shall see, but in commenting on the advantage it was to have met so much opposition, she summed up the temper of Burgos very well. "Since this place is a kingdom, perhaps it wouldn't have noticed us had we entered silently." Mother Teresa's instinctive insight at its keenest!

Just as it was the Lord who started something in Galilee many centuries ago, so it was here: it was the encouragement He gave that enabled Teresa not to give in. "Be sure to make both of these foundations," He said, referring to Palencia and Burgos.

And yet it appeared initially as if this would be an easy task. Take the archbishop to whom they looked for permission. Archbishop Cristóbal Vela was not only a native of Avila and well acquainted with Teresa's work; he was a relative and near neighbour who knew the family well.

He had formerly been a professor at Salamanca, then

(from 1575) bishop in the Canary Islands and had become archbishop of Burgos in 1580. The famous seminary he founded there was proof of his zeal.

It was precisely on the occasion of his installation as archbishop, when he was receiving the pallium from Bishop Alvaro de Mendoza, that the latter broached the subject of a Carmelite house in Burgos. On that occasion not only did he agree, he was positively pleased: ''He had wanted one of these monasteries, because he knew how well the Lord was served in them'' (F. 31,3). No sign of a threat from this quarter, then.

Another favourable factor in the undertaking was Teresa's close friendship with a rich and noble lady of that city, called Doña Catalina de Tolosa. This devout widow had two sons and six daughters, and such was her love for Carmel that all of these, except one daughter who died young, entered the Discalced Carmelites.

Here Teresa could count not only on Doña Catalina, her fortune and her family, but on her friends as well. There was Fr. Ripalda of the Society of Jesus, Doña María Manrique and her daughter, a son of hers who held a prominent position on the City Council, and several other good and faithful servants of the Lord whose names we shall have occasion to mention presently.

So, with the required backing of her Order and favourable prospects, the wheels of this new venture were set in motion.

They weren't well started before two apparently formidable obstacles raised their heads. The first concerned the permission of the City Council. They had not sought this, but now the archbishop insisted on

The cloister in St. Augustine's Convent.

it, lest they encounter the kind of trouble they had had in Avila. The second was the fact that they had no endowment to guarantee an income.

It is worth recalling, perhaps, that the objections sometimes raised by cities to monasteries which relied on alms were not prompted by any dislike of the nuns themselves, but by the fear that they would cause less alms to be given to other communities and all would suffer as a result. Opposition from bishops was on the same grounds; they preferred to refuse

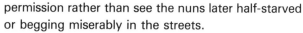

Fuente de la Flora, where St. Teresa stayed on her arrival in Burgos, in the home of doña Catalina de Tolosa.

Façade of the Hospital of the Conception.

permission rather than see the nuns later half-starved or begging miserably in the streets.

These two difficulties were taken care of by the good ladies mentioned above. Doña Catalina and Doña María prevailed upon the latter's son to raise the matter of their permission with the Council.

In the Council's Minute Book there is the following entry for 4 November 1581:

"Having heard what Don Alonso has proposed, they said that permission will be granted as requested, since this work is so pious and necessary for this city."

Three days later Doña Catalina signed a document in which she guaranteed the maintenance of the new community. "They shall have," it ran, "sufficient for their support, because I, for the service of Our Lord and the good of this city, will give them a house to live in, and I will see to their maintenance whenever necessary." Such generosity must have left Teresa speechless.

People were now advising that she move quickly; there was talk of others wanting to found in Burgos too. Teresa was doubtful if her health could stand the rigours of a Burgos winter, so she decided to send the prioress of Palencia in her stead. The Lord thought otherwise: "One day... when raising this whole matter before the Lord... He said: 'Pay no attention to the cold; I am the true warmth. The devil is marshalling all his forces against this foundation; you marshal mine

Garden and convent in Burgos.

The Saint's well, in the Burgos convent.

in its favour, and make sure you go personally for it will prove very beneficial'" (F. 31,11).

The only person who didn't think everything was now perfectly straightforward was Fr. Gracián. He was provincial superior, and he insisted that Mother Teresa obtain the archbishop's permission in writing. She wrote again to her friends in Burgos and they assured her that the matter had been sufficiently discussed with that Prelate. Gracián relented, but only on condition that he would go with them in case any unforeseen difficulty should arise. How right he was!

On January 2nd they left Avila; Teresa took along her niece Teresita, and two nuns from Alba, one of them Tomasina Bautista, the new prioress.

The first leg of the journey was in driving sleet and snow. Teresa arrived in Medina "very tired and ill, with a large sore in her throat. She could eat only a little boiled mutton." Yet her own illness and fever was no obstacle to her healing others; her very presence cured the prioress of a fever which had kept her confined to bed and healed Sr. Ana's cancer of the nose. Then it was on to Valladolid. Teresa could barely speak, but she strongly approved of her sisters taking charge of a college for girls which a generous gentleman was anxious to endow. "Nothing serves the Lord better," she said, "than colleges where girls can be educated in recollection, virtue and prayer. When they are brought up that way, God calls many

St. Teresa's cell.

Christ during His Passion. Picture in the Saint's cell (Burgos).

of them to be nuns, and those who marry... make their husbands, children and the whole family good." Unfortunately, this initiative never got off the ground; the Abbot of Valladolid insisted on its being under his jurisdiction.

Valladolid is a damp place and Teresa moved on quickly to Palencia, where she received a rapturous welcome. When, after a six-day stay, she wanted to proceed, all about her protested that the roads were impassable. That inner Voice, however, whispered: "It is alright to go; I will be with you."

Trusting in this word, but keeping it to herself, Teresa moved on. Seventeen leagues to Burgos, and everyone thought them extremely rash. They are now eight nuns, three friars, the bursar of Palencia cathedral, and some inexperienced mule drivers.

If we were to describe in detail the misadventures and dangers of this journey we would never end. Sometimes the wagons stuck fast in the deep sticky mud. There was the time the nuns thought Fr. Gracián had fallen off his horse in the river; another when he thought Mother Teresa's wagon was being taken away by the current; and more than once the mule boys had to hold on to a wagon wheel for dear life to prevent a wagon from overturning.

Nevertheless, they advanced from one village to another, from one inn to another. In one of the latter, we are told, there wasn't even room to put Mother Teresa to bed.

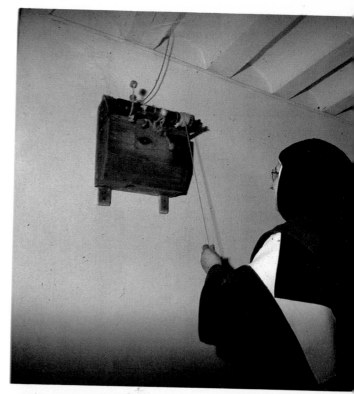

And the worst was still to come. When they reached the pontoon bridge over the Arlanzón near Buniel, the river had become a veritable sea on all sides. Here their collective fears and anxiety reached their peak. The pontoons were narrow and well-covered with water, so they hired a guide to see them across. All a wagon had to do here was veer a little to right or left and it would have been swept away. This is how Anne of St. Bartholomew, Mother Teresa's nurse, described the crossing:

"Before entering this danger we went to confession, asked our Mother to bless us, and recited the Creed, just like people who were about to die. Seeing how discouraged we were, the Saint laughed at us and said: 'Come on, daughters, what more could you ask for than to be martyrs here for the love of Our Lord?' Then she said that she would go first. If she drowned we were to turn back. In the end it pleased God to deliver us from this danger."

This must have happened about noon on January 26th. By mid-afternoon they had reached Burgos, but they made a detour to visit the famous Cristo de Burgos. They may have thought it better not to enter in the full light of day and were therefore just killing time. But it is not unreasonable to suppose that Teresa would have liked to pay a last visit to that impressive image of the crucified Christ which must have aroused all her memories and great love of the Sacred Humanity.

EN ESTE SITIO ESTABA LA PIEZA Y EL NICHO EN LA PARED, CON LA INSCRIPCION QUE AUN DESPUES DE ARRUINADO EL CONVENTO SE LEIA EN ESTA FORMA. EL DIA DE LA ASCENSION 24 DE MAYO DEL AÑO DE 1582, CRECIO TANTO EL RIO QUE INUNDO LA CIUDAD COMO UN DILUVIO, LAS GENTES AFLIGIDAS CON LAS RUINAS DESAMPARABAN LAS CASAS Y LAS RELIGIOSAS SUS MONASTERIOS, LA Sª MADRE, CONFIADA EN LA DIVINA PROVIDENCIA, NO LO CONSINTIO EN SU NUEVO CONVENTO, MANDO SUBIR A COLOCAR EN ESTE NICHO AL SEÑOR SACRAMENTADO, SE QUEDO CON SUS HIJAS ROGANDO POR EL REMEDIO, Y LAS AGUAS CEDIERON CON FELICIDAD TAN GRANDE, QUE ADMIRADOS EL Sª ARZOBISPO Y OTROS PERSONAGES, LO CREYERON PRODIGIO DE LA Sª FUNDADORA.

After all, one day long ago she had had her Damascus experience. A real and personal encounter with Christ had changed her whole life.

Teresa's Christ was no dimly perceived refraction of a mystery; He was real. He was the Christ of the biblical scenes that so fascinated her. He was the Christ of the Eucharist where she saw him as clearly as his contemporaries had, whom she adored hidden there, with whom she could do business, especially just after Communion. He was at once her Master and Friend. He was the Christ who was involved and identified with that Church so burdened with problems and evils, conflicts and defeats. He was the Christ of her inner life.

I'm sure she didn't spend her time wondering where this crucifix came from, or admiring its impressive realism. Impressed she no doubt was, but she would have gone beyond the image to God's infinite love reflected in it. She had allowed herself to become involved in this great drama herself, allowed God to go on loving man through her.

But, to return to our story. One would have thought that with that infernal journey behind them, the devil's opposition would be at an end. Teresa tells us the turn which events took during their first twenty-four hours in Burgos:

"It had been decided to proceed with the foundation immediately, and I had brought several letters from Canon Salinas (in Palencia) to his relatives and friends urging them to help us.

"And so they did. They came next day... to inquire how they could be of service. Since our only anxiety had been about the City Council, we thought everything ought to go smoothly now. Since no one yet knew of our arrival (because the rain had been so heavy when we reached Doña Catalina's house) we thought it would be as well to inform the archbishop of our arrival, so that we could then say the first Mass, as is my custom nearly everywhere. The weather prevented this.

"That night we rested in welcome comfort, thanks to this holy woman. Actually it did not do me any good; the great fire she put down to dry our clothes... affected me so much that next day I could not even raise my head. I spoke from my bed to those who came. We put a veil over an internal window of bars for the purpose. Being a day on which it was essential to attend to business, this was very trying.

"In the morning the Fr. Provincial went to ask the archbishop's blessing; we thought there would be no more to it than that. But he found him so angry at my coming without his permission that one would never have thought he had requested this himself.... So he spoke of me in very angry terms to our Fr. Provincial. When he was forced to admit that it was he who had told me to come, he said that was only to discuss the matter with me alone, and not with so many nuns.

"He dismissed the Fr. Provincial and told him that if we didn't have revenues and a house of our own he would not grant his permission and that we could go back to where we had come from" (F. 31, 18-21).

Teresa's comment on all of this was "with the roads in such a fine state, and the weather so suitable!" We've seen the condition in which the roads were; the archbishop's disposition was apparently no better.

What bothered Teresa was not so much the conditions he laid down as the protracted negotiations and the delay all this would involve.

For the present, Doña Catalina's house became their convent. Since it had one rather fine room, which the Jesuits had used as a chapel when they first came to

Burgos, they asked the archbishop if they could have Mass there. He would not allow Mass in a private house, he said.

This meant that the community had to go to Mass on Sundays and Holy Days in the nearest church in the bleak Burgos winter.

Meanwhile, Teresa's friends were not idle. Canon Manso kept up the pressure on the archbishop, but the only answer he got was an impatient expression of surprise at the nuns being still in Burgos. Doña Catalina decided that a positive step would be to transfer ownership of her house to Mother Teresa and let her turn it into a monastery. The archbishop's officials dithered about for a month and then pronounced the house unsuitable because of the damp and its proximity to a noisy street. The same people refused to accept that Doña Catalina could maintain the community; they laid down 40,000 ducats as a minimum guarantee.

No wonder the Lord had insisted on Teresa's coming in person! The devil appeared to be having a field day. The Lord's word in the midst of these disappointments was: "Now, Teresa, stand fast."

By now Lent was approaching and Fr. Gracián had preaching commitments in Valladolid. He couldn't bear to see the sisters tramping the muddy streets to Mass, so before he left he sought some way of remedying this situation. With the help of some interested parties in the civil administration, he succeeded in obtaining an attic for them in the Hospital of the Immaculate Conception.

So, on February 23rd, almost a month after their arrival, they moved their belongings to this new abode. It was poor, but at least they could now attend Mass from a balcony overlooking the hospital chapel, and create their own convent atmosphere in the attic.

Burgos convent: high altar reredos.

Teresa never forgot the generosity of the lady who fed them all for a month "as if they were all her children."

Teresa had more time now for house-hunting and collecting money. She also paid frequent visits to the hospital patients and other religious communities in the city. Her simplicity and cheerfulness captivated people wherever she went. In fact two nuns from another convent insisted on joining her little community.

Negotiations continued. Before he left Burgos, Fr. Gracián enlisted the help of an old friend in the medical profession, D. Antonio Aguiar, in the task of finding Mother Teresa a house. A difficult task as the depopulation of Burgos had not yet begun. After several disappointments he struck gold: the Mansino property was being put up for sale. The Mother was called, and both agreed that it was ideal. What would they be asking? she wondered. Once again that unmistakable "voice" took her to task: "Are you letting money hold you up?" The price, they discovered, was most reasonable, and they quickly and with great secrecy concluded the purchase.

The conveyance was signed on March 12th. By the 18th the community had taken up residence. The total cost, that is for "two houses, yards, gardens and fruit trees," was 1,290 ducats, payable over twelve months. The nuns had got a real bargain, and many were soon wondering how they had not come to hear of it. The owners were criticised for having let it go so cheaply, but they were quite happy to see their property become a monastery. St. Teresa was delighted, and even the archbishop claimed some credit — he had forced them to look for a house!

He was pleased enough to visit the community, but not, it would seem, to part with the long sought permission to celebrate Mass in it. So for a little while more the sisters had to repair to the nearest church for Mass.

On April 18th the prelate finally gave in. "He granted Dr. Manso permission to say Mass there the following day and reserve the Blessed Sacrament." The Prior of the Dominican community "said the High Mass, to the accompaniment of many minstrels, who came uninvited" (F. 31,45).

Teresa brings this long account to an end as if she had been telling a fairy tale. The joy that another oasis had been founded knows no bounds. Here is how she concludes the story of her last foundation:

"All our friends were very happy. In fact, so was most of the city, for many had been moved to pity by our plight... The joy of Doña Catalina de Tolosa and all the sisters was such that I was moved to devotion, and I said to God: 'Lord, as you see, all these servants of yours want is to serve you and see themselves enclosed for your sake in a place they will never leave.'... Some days after the monastery had been founded the Fr. Provincial and I agreed that there were certain drawbacks to the endowment Doña Catalina had given this house. We put our trust in God and returned the money to her, without letting the archbishop know....

"I did not want to leave until I saw whether there were persons desirous of entering this monastery. One day, after Communion, I was wondering about this, and the Lord said: 'What are you wondering about? The work here is finished and you can safely go away.' From this I understood that they would lack nothing... I got ready to leave, because I felt I was only enjoying myself in this house. I might have more trouble elsewhere, but I would also do more good" (F. 31, 45-49).

Teresa departed, but she had left her mark on Burgos. Some reminders of her physical presence there: a wall in the garden in which one can still see the window of her cell, the cell itself, the well, and a portion of the church. Among the relics are a letter of hers, a veil, an *alpargata,* a jewel casket which Doña Catalina gave her, and some pictures.

The author of our drawings, Hye Hoys, drawing the last of the series in the Saint's cell in Alba.

ALBA DE TORMES: JOURNEY'S END

Mother Teresa must have been feeling really tired, she had probably decided that Madrid, her cherished dream, would be the last foundation she would personally make. Now, duty called her to Avila, where she was still prioress, for the profession of her niece Teresita, who was with her in Burgos.

Her presence in Burgos was not exactly superfluous, but neither was it necessary. So, about 26 July 1581, the feast of her beloved St. Anne, she set out with her niece and her nurse for Avila.

First a stop at Palencia, where her health gave no cause for alarm. She remained on here until mid-September. Then she moved on to Medina del Campo. Here an order from Fr. Antonio de Jesús, acting provincial in Fr. Gracián's absence, awaited her. She was to make a detour through Alba de Tormes because the Duchess of Alba wanted to meet her again and have her pray for the safe confinement of her daughter-in-law. All who were present on that occasion agree that this was one of the most difficult acts of obedience that Teresa had ever had to make, for by now she was really ill again.

The journey from Medina to Alba was in the usual covered wagon, a serious risk to her life. The nurse found the journey a real torment, for she could not find nourishing food. "When I saw that money could not buy what we needed, I couldn't look at our Mother without crying. She was like a corpse... And all we had to give her were some figs... While I was sobbing at seeing her in such great need... she comforted me saying the figs were delicious, that there

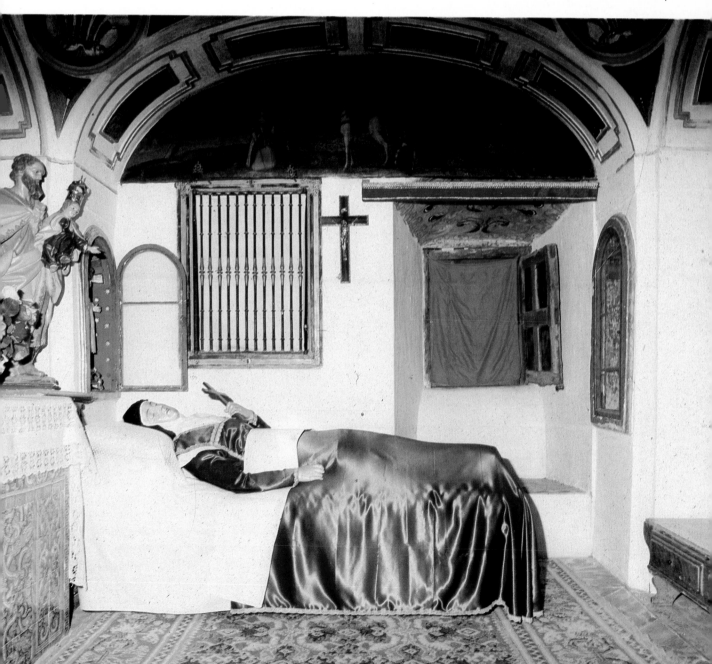

Cell in which the Saint died in the Carmelite convent of Alba, now converted into an oratory.

The Saint's tomb.

were many poor people who couldn't enjoy such nice things.''

At last they reached Alba. The sisters knew how ill she was and were waiting anxiously. They would have loved to chat with her, but they had the good sense to put her to bed immediately. ''God help me,'' she said, ''how tired I feel! In twenty years I've never had to go to bed as early as this.''

On September 29th she took to her bed, never to rise again. She knew death was near and prepared herself to receive it.

October 3rd came. The sisters were praying and weeping by her bedside. Fr. Antonio administered the last rites of the Church. The Duchess was in constant attendance, serving what little food she took, giving her medicine, even making her bed.

But there was no containing this illness. Between bouts of total collapse, loss of speech, violent changes in pulse rate, Teresa, her voice trembling and getting weaker by the minute, dictated her last testament.

According to her nurse, ''She asked for the Blessed Sacrament.... When they were taking it away she sat up in the bed with a great surge of spirit and said joyfully: 'My Lord, it is time to be going. Very well, Your Will be done.'

''She thanked God unceasingly that she was a daughter of the Church and was dying in it. She said she hoped for salvation through the merits of Christ, and asked us all to pray God to forgive her sins and to regard his own mercy rather than them....

''On the evening of the day she died Fr. Antonio told

me to go and get myself something to eat. I had no sooner left than the Holy Mother became very restless and began looking all about her. The Father asked if she wanted me back and she nodded. They called me and when she saw me she smiled at me. She affectionately took my hands and laid her head between my arms. I held her there until she died."

It was 4 October 1582. Teresa was 67 years old.

Today her body lies in the convent chapel at Alba, and through a little window to one side of the altar one can view the room in which she died.

In 1584, when Fr. Gracián was making a visitation, her tomb was opened. In spite of the large quantity of stones and chalk that had been thrown on top of the coffin, the body was as fresh and whole as if it had only just been buried.

In 1585, the General Chapter of the Discalced Carmelites decreed that the body be transferred to St. Joseph's, Avila. This was carried out on 25 November of that year. The Duke of Alba, however, petitioned Pope Sixtus IV to have the body returned to Alba. So the following August back it went again.

So great was the fame of her sanctity that the juridical procedures for beatification began soon after her death. She was beatified on 24 April 1614, and canonized on 12 March 1622 by Pope Gregory XV, in the company of St. Isidore, St. Ignatius of Loyola, St. Francis Xavier, and St. Philip Neri.

Her remains are preserved in a silver urn presented by King Ferdinand IV and his queen Doña Bárbara de Braganza, whose body, encased in a black marble urn, is also preserved here.

SAINT TERESA'S WRITINGS

The Saint's writings concern her own life, and her teaching on the spiritual and monastic life. None of her books was written by choice; she wrote only on the orders of her superiors and confessors.

These books have gone into thousands of editions in a wide variety of languages. The first Spanish edition was edited by Fray Luis de León in 1588. Here is how he introduced it:

"I doubt if anything has been written in our language to equal these writings for purity and ease of style, for happy choice of words, and an unaffected elegance which is so entirely pleasing. Whenever I read them I am filled anew with admiration. To mention only two of the many benefits to be derived from reading them, they make virtue attractive and set the reader on fire with love of Teresa and love of God."

Her principal writings are:

THE BOOK OF HER LIFE

This is her longest work. Its forty chapters flow easily and simply along as she describes the favours she had received from the Lord up to the time of writing. It was written by order of her confessors between 1562 and 1565. The original is preserved in El Escorial, the famous monastic library near Madrid.

THE WAY OF PERFECTION

This was written in 1566 and 1567 while she was still at St. Joseph's, Avila. It could be described as a kind of spiritual Constitution of her Order: it teaches them their mission in life, how to make their life and prayer interchangeable, and the particular importance for them of virtues such as humility, charity and detachment. Teresa rewrote this book herself later. The first version is preserved in El Escorial; the second in the Valladolid Carmel.

CONCEPTIONS OF THE LOVE OF GOD

This short collection of reflections begins with thoughts on the reverence with which Sacred Scripture should be read. It also touches on true peace and more advanced stages of prayer. Teresa's original manuscript is no longer extant. A confessor of hers told her to throw it in the fire, and she promptly did so. However, the nuns had already made copies of it, and from these it was published in 1611.

THE INTERIOR CASTLE

Teresa began this book — also sometimes known by the alternative title of *The Mansions* — on 2 June 1577. She stopped writing a month later, but was able to finish it in Avila on 20 November of the same year. This is her masterpiece, both from a literary and a spiritual standpoint. In it she likens the soul to a castle in which there are many apartments. The Lord of the castle is God, who dwells in the innermost apartments. Spiritual progress is seen in terms of movement towards this centre.

The original manuscript is in the Seville Carmel.

RELATIONS

This is a collection of unconnected reports on her own inner state. The originals of various reports are scattered rather widely, the most substantial collection of them being at St. Joseph's, Avila.

EXCLAMATIONS

Reminiscent of St. Augustine's *Soliloquies,* these outpourings of fervent love for God were written at various times. They were first published by Luis de León in 1588.

POEMS

These little poems were never meant for publication; she wrote them either to entertain her sisters or to celebrate some event, and made no claims to poetic talent. A few, however, have acquired some standing.

THE BOOK OF FOUNDATIONS

This was written as the monasteries were being founded. Its documentary importance is indisputable, but its pages are also a treasure house of spiritual and psychological digressions. As she narrates the various happenings with the simplicity that goes with genius, the reader is impressed by the divine atmosphere that pervades the tale and by the great humanity and practicality of this woman whom one tends to associate too closely perhaps with the truly extraordinary aspects of a life lived in such close intimacy with God. Heavenly she certainly was, but she was also down-to-earth.
The original manuscript is in El Escorial.

GUIDELINES FOR THE VISITATION OF CONVENTS

This short work seeks to advise both nuns and their visiting superiors on how to make a visitation

Relic of the Saint's incorrupt left arm (Carmelite convent, Alba de Tormes).

spiritually profitable. Fr. Gracián asked her to write this, feeling that her wide experience would be an invaluable guide to others. She wrote it in Toledo in 1576. The original is in El Escorial.

LETTERS

It has been calculated that in the last twenty years of her life Teresa must have written between fifteen and twenty thousand letters. Only five hundred or so have survived. Though addressed to a great variety of people, from family to King, they are all charmingly simple and spontaneous. Their clarity and sincerity show a talented and big-hearted woman.

DOCTOR OF THE CHURCH

As if to authenticate all that has been said above, on 15 October 1967 Pope Paul announced his intention of declaring St. Teresa a ''Doctor of the Universal Church.''
This unexpected announcement was a complete surprise because hitherto no woman had ever been accorded this official distinction.
In fact the first person to be surprised at what flowed from Teresa's pen was herself. ''I see clearly,'' she confessed, ''that it is not I who am saying this; I don't arrange it in my mind and afterwards I don't know how I succeeded in saying it'' (L. 14,8). And elsewhere: ''Many of the things I write here do not come out of my head; my heavenly Master has been saying them'' (L. 39,8).

The appointed day arrived: 27 September 1970. Pope Paul VI, in the presence of official delegations from all over the world and of thousands of the faithful, made this solemn pronouncement:
''THEREFORE, IN COMPLETE CERTAINTY AND AFTER MATURE DELIBERATION, WITH THE FULLNESS OF THE APOSTOLIC AUTHORITY, WE PROCLAIM SAINT TERESA OF JESUS, VIRGIN FROM AVILA, DOCTOR OF THE UNIVERSAL CHURCH.''
With the placing of this supreme seal on her ''message,'' her travels were truly at an end.

Relic of the Saint's heart (Alba de Tormes, Carmelite nuns).

Contents

TRANSLATOR'S NOTE

The numerous quotations from St. Teresa's Works in this book have been translated afresh from the original. The abbreviated form of reference after each quotation is to be understood as follows: the letter stands for a book, the first number for a chapter, the second number for a paragraph. The books quoted from are abbreviated thus:

L   : The Book of Her Life.
WP: The Way of Perfection.
F   : The Book of the Foundations.

Statue of St. Teresa (Noviciado Compañía de Santa Teresa. Avila). ▷

Copyright of this edition for text: © Editorial Monte Carmelo - Burgos (Spain).

Photographs: Il Messagero del S. Bambino Gesù di Praga - Arenzano (Italia). Editorial Escudo de Oro, S.A. - Barcelona. P. Girolamo Salvatico. Editorial Monte Carmelo - Burgos (España).

2nd Edition, October 1982

I.S.B.N.

English 84-378-0845-6

Dep. Legal B. 24671-XXV

Impreso en España - Printed in Spain
F.I.S.A. Palaudarias, 26 - Barcelona-4